Accountability Is the Key

Unlocking School Potential through Enhanced Educational Leadership

John Hunt

ROWMAN & LITTLEFIELD EDUCATION
A division of
ROWMAN & LITTLEFIELD
Lanham • Boulder • New York • Toronto • Plymouth, UK

Published by Rowman & Littlefield Education
A division of Rowman & Littlefield
4501 Forbes Boulevard, Suite 200, Lanham, Maryland 20706
www.rowman.com

10 Thornbury Road, Plymouth PL6 7PP, United Kingdom

Copyright © 2014 by John Hunt

All rights reserved. No part of this book may be reproduced in any form or by any electronic or mechanical means, including information storage and retrieval systems, without written permission from the publisher, except by a reviewer who may quote passages in a review.

British Library Cataloguing in Publication Information Available

Library of Congress Cataloging-in-Publication Data

Hunt, John, 1948–
Accountability is the key : unlocking school potential through enhanced educational leadership / John Hunt.
pages cm.
Includes bibliographical references and index.
ISBN 978-1-4758-0465-2 (cloth : alk. paper)—ISBN 978-1-4758-0466-9 (pbk. : alk. paper)—ISBN 978-1-4758-0467-6 (electronic : alk. paper)
1. Educational accountability. 2. Educational leadership. 3. Motivation in education. 4. Academic achievement. I. Title.
LB2806.22.H86 2013
371.14'4—dc23
2013030911

∞™ The paper used in this publication meets the minimum requirements of American National Standard for Information Sciences Permanence of Paper for Printed Library Materials, ANSI/NISO Z39.48-1992.

Printed in the United States of America

Contents

Preface v
Acknowledgments vii

1 The Current World 1
2 Why Money Matters 17
3 The Shadow System 35
4 Administrative Decision Making: Conflict or Consensus? 55
5 Listening Skills: The Administrator's Best Friend 75
6 The Future of Administrative Accountability: Friend or Foe? 95

References 117
Index 121

Preface

The author's first administrative position was that of junior high principal in a building in which the student enrollment was 75 percent minority and 90 percent of the students were eligible for free and reduced lunch. In subsequent years, he served as the director of two separate K–12 university laboratory schools, as an instructional director in relatively large school districts, and finally, ended his public school career as a superintendent. While he worked low-income districts, blue-collar districts, and affluent suburban districts, there was one constant—the increasing demand for accountability from constituents and from the legislature. The calls for accountability have continued.

Early in the author's administrative career, teachers and administrators were generally held in high regard by the public. However, that began to change, in the fourth year of his administrative career, with the publication of A Nation at Risk (1983). That report called into question the effectiveness of U.S. public schools and initiated at least three waves of public school reform; each with its own form of administrative accountability. He retired from the superintendency three years after the passage of the No Child Left Behind Act (2002) but immediately began teaching school administration to prospective principals and superintendents at a Midwestern university. Based upon daily interactions with public school administrators, it is clear the calls for administrative accountability are more strident today than they ever were during the author's administrative career.

The purpose of this book is to examine the current state of public education and to honestly review what the critics are saying about public schools framed in the context of accountability. This includes a look at the present trend toward resegregation and a movement toward a two-class system in this country. The evolution of the definition of administrative accountability is outlined and the shadow system instrumental in framing the current definition is exposed. The shadow system includes vouchers, charter schools, and the phenomenal growth of homeschooling. Perhaps most important in this area has been the successful attempt to sway public education policy by private individuals and groups. They have accomplished this through the use of their personal and corporate resources.

Voices from the field, particularly those of current administrators and school board members, are considered as the administrative skills needed to navigate the shoals of accountability are examined. The ability of administrators to successfully engage in conflict resolution and to manage critical situations has never been more essential than today. The specific human relations and communications skills needed to handle crises and to successfully answer the calls for accountability are addressed. Suggestions for topics for inclusion in educational administration preparation programs and administrative in-service programs, with an eye towards meeting these needs, are provided. Key among these is an increased emphasis on listening skills.

The book concludes with a call to reframe the definition of accountability. It gives recommendations regarding how administrators can regain the mantle of "educational expert" and details the skills needed by today's generation of school building and school district administrators. Among the suggestions is the call for educational administrators to form partnerships with all other public school educators. The need for educational administrators to become much more politically active, beginning at the grassroots level is addressed. The author also calls for a redistribution of federal funds to support research regarding urban school effectiveness and to provide pay incentives to entice the best teachers and administrators to work in the neediest districts.

Acknowledgments

First, the author would like to recognize the sacrifices in family time made by his wife, Karen, and their daughters, Elizabeth, Stephanie, and Rebekah, due to his administrative career. Not only did his career require missing family activities, but it also resulted in multiple moves over the years. He also needs to acknowledge the many great school and district administrators with whom he worked throughout his career. These individuals served as his mentors, his examples, and his sources of inspiration. Much of his success as an administrator should be attributed to these individuals.

He spent nine years as an instructional director in three large districts where his primary role was to monitor, supervise, and evaluate building-level principals. This relationship with principals continued when he became a superintendent. One of the primary lessons he learned from these fine principals was that differing administrative styles can be successful in differing locations. He also served under a number of excellent superintendents and assistant or associate superintendents, and watching them operate gave him a "toolkit" of excellent strategies that he employed when he became a superintendent. Finally, he was gratified with the relationships he developed with school board members over the eleven years he served as superintendent.

Specifically, the author would like to honor the contributions of the following individuals, some now deceased, to his administrative career: Vickie Axton, Andrea Brown, Robert L. Buser, Cile Chavez, H. Mack Clark, Tom Crawford, Vicky Cullinan, Darrell Dick, Cathy Eddy, Gary Fields, Don Gossett, Ken Hill, Dan Kern, Kevin Koch, Theresa Kovach, Robert Oakes, Gregory N. Pierson, Jim Skeeters, Suzanne Skeeters, Norman Stremsterfer, Maureen Talbert, Steve Turner, Gary Volling, Donald Wachter, Walt Warfield, and Kathy Wilson. A special thanks is given for the research conducted by one of the graduate students in the Department of Educational Leadership at Southern Illinois University Edwardsville, Natalia Garcia. Without her assistance, this book would have taken much longer to write. The author would like to acknowledge the excellent work currently being conducted by America's educational administrators—they are a continuing source of inspiration to him. Finally, this book is dedicated to the author's grandchildren, Isabelle, John, and Violet.

ONE

The Current World

How did we arrive at the situation that administrators find themselves in today, with administrative accountability reduced to how well students perform on achievement tests? In an increasing number of states, teachers are now being at least partially evaluated on how well their students perform on mandated state tests. The same is true for principals in some locations. It is likely that superintendents, with an additional degree of separation from students, will be next.

The immediate answer to the question posed above is related to the implementation of the Race to the Top (RTTT) program in 2009. The genesis of this program was embedded within the American Recovery and Reinvestment Act (ARRA) of 2009. Since a major portion of the scoring rubric for RTTT applications was related to improving teacher and principal performance, this led to a flurry of activity, with a number of states passing legislation linking student achievement to the evaluation of professional educators. The implication is that accountability should be primarily judged by how well students perform on state-developed tests. Whether this implication is valid is addressed later in the book. First, it is important to review the evolution of the definition of accountability in this country.

THE EXCELLENCE MOVEMENT

The first of the reform movements, commonly referred to as the Excellence Movement, dates back to the 1980s. This movement was mainly driven by state legislatures and state departments of education and was seen as a top-down movement by administrators. This was a time of experimenting with the conditions of teaching. It was not unusual for schools and districts to expand hours of instruction and the length of the school year. Some states increased teacher certification requirements. Educators also experimented with both the frequency and types of student assessment.

Several states passed educational reform packages during this era. Many of these states were in the South with governors such as Lamar Alexander, Bill Clinton, and Richard Riley playing key roles in this process. While there was a push for administrators to become more engaged in leadership as opposed to management, the primary focus of this movement was on the education system as a whole, rather than what was happening in individual districts, schools, and classrooms. Business interests were able to strongly influence state legislatures during this time, and this filtered down to the public schools. Both building level and district administrators were urged to read books promoting business practices and to mimic these practices in their schools and districts. It is ironic that most of these books promoted management rather than leadership.

THE RESTRUCTURING MOVEMENT

A few years later, the Restructuring Movement emerged. Unlike the Excellence Movement, much of this movement transpired at the school-district level. Educators and their associations backed this movement, which promoted site-based management. This was a time when superintendents and school boards were asked to share larger amounts of control with the individual schools in their districts. This often manifested itself in calls to turn over much of the budgetary authority to individual principals and schools. This led to increased public scrutiny of principals and superintendents.

The enhanced focus on the building level increased the need for flexibility and creativity on the part of building principals. Not only were principals encouraged to be open to new approaches and ideas, but the same was expected of teachers. Principals were expected to possess the skills to coax teachers to improve their professional practice. If principals did not have these skills, they were expected to become experts in instructional leadership in fairly short order.

This era of restructuring called for a new worldview by administrators. Superintendents were asked to become comfortable with, or at least accept, relinquishing some of their power to the educators in the buildings in their districts. It was clearly an exciting time for principals, who were definitively asked to become instructional leaders and who were encouraged to experiment with a variety of new approaches and educational practices. However, the axiom says that into every life some rain must fall. With the new flexibility given to schools and districts came demands for enhanced accountability from legislators and constituents.

For the first time ever, many states began to require the public reporting of student achievement outcomes during this period. Often, this led to school-by-school and district-to-district comparisons of test results in the area press. This very public manifestation of school and district student achievement led to a type of accountability that heightened the anxiety level of many administrators and caused some to begin seriously examining student achievement in the quest for strategies for improving student performance.

THE STANDARDS MOVEMENT

The most recent of the three movements, which continues in a modified form today, is the Standards Movement. This movement, which was given an additional boost by the signing of the No Child Left Behind Act (NCLB) in 2002, has diverted public attention away from the activities of teachers to the achievement of students. There have been positive elements resulting from the implementation of NCLB. It has now become common practice to focus on the academic performance of the various subgroups in our schools. Educators are now very aware of the performance of students from minority groups, from low-income families, and with specific learning difficulties.

Prior to NCLB, it was not unusual for administrators to review achievement data without examining the performance of subgroups. If students in a particular building or district were performing at or above the regional, state, and national levels, administrators were typically happy. The situation was somewhat like the individual with her head in the oven and her feet in the freezer—on average, she was okay. This approach is no longer acceptable.

Another impact of the Standards Movement was to cause building-level administrators to become much more involved in school-improvement planning. Rather than addressing student progress globally, educators began to target student achievement in specific subject areas. With the advent of NCLB, this increasingly became a focus on the areas tested for Academic Yearly Progress (AYP) purposes. One study (Hunt, 2006) showed that both school improvement planning and staff development in those districts not making AYP were beginning to concentrate almost exclusively on reading, mathematics and test-taking skills. Another major national study (Rentner et al., 2006) indicated that 71 percent of the elementary districts analyzed were reducing time allocated to subjects other than reading or mathematics, or were eliminating some of the "non-tested" subjects from the curriculum of their schools.

Basing accountability primarily upon how well students perform on state-level tests has led to numerous philosophical and ethical issues for administrators. For example, a particular district may decide that placing all of its elementary English Language Learner (ELL) students in one elementary school may make educational sense. Staff, materials and efforts could be concentrated in one particular building. However, since ELL students may initially struggle with state-mandated testing, and because concentrating all ELL students in one elementary building might cause them to constitute a subgroup for that building for AYP purposes, what should the district do? Should it do what was initially thought to be educationally sound and keep the children in one building, or should it disperse the students to their home schools in an attempt to protect the "reputation" of one elementary building? In either case, if the ELL students fail to make AYP as a group, the district will be judged as not meeting AYP in this area.

Another ethical dilemma for many districts involves the federal Title I program. The federal sanctions for failing to make AYP in a school designated as Title I are much more severe than in a non–Title I school. Typically, school districts have some discretion regarding the manner in which they distribute Title I funds. Since Title I funds are limited, districts are quite judicious in how they allocate these scarce federal dollars. Historically, many districts have decided to concentrate the funding in the lower grade levels in the belief that student deficiencies should be addressed while students are still young and while the learning deficits are still relatively small.

However, as schools began failing to meet AYP, it was not unusual for the first of these to be high schools and middle schools. In some regions, grant money was made available to assist schools in their staff development efforts in the attempt to improve student achievement. The issue with this funding was that these high schools and middle schools would need to be designated Title I buildings, which would subsequently place them in greater jeopardy of stiff sanctions. Many administrators struggled with these issues as they worked to meet the challenges of improving student achievement. Accepting the funds often increased the possibility of sanctions.

Initially, the approach taken to improving student achievement was often related to a school's AYP status. Diamond and Spillane (2004) conducted a study of four Chicago elementary schools; two of which were making AYP and two that were not. In the schools that were making AYP, school improvement efforts and staff development were still broadly based and addressed subjects beyond the tested areas. However, in the two schools struggling with AYP, efforts were much more targeted and a great deal of emphasis was placed on the "bubble kids." In the other school, all children received the benefits of the teachers' efforts in this area. The issue of "bubble kids" is not just isolated to two Chicago elementary schools; it has become a national phenomenon.

THE BUBBLE KIDS

Meeting the accountability challenge has become a daunting task for many building and school district administrators. Facing an AYP bar that gets steadily higher as 2014 approaches, and dealing with limited resources with an increasingly poorer and more diverse student clientele in many districts, administrators seem to have their backs against a wall. Many administrators could liken their situation to a triage setting in a hospital emergency room. In order to deal with a critical situation, some administrators have been selective in which students they target for special attention and assistance. These students have become known as the "bubble kids." They are the students on the bubble between meeting and not meeting AYP. Since it is thought that with special focus and assistance, these students can improve their state assessment test performance just enough to meet AYP standards, increasing numbers of schools and school districts have been concentrating their efforts on this segment of the school population.

What happens to the other students in this bubble approach to accountability? It is often assumed that the advanced learners and gifted need no additional assistance and that they will be fine and will naturally progress. This could not be further from the truth. We expect these students to be our future leaders, and if we do not challenge them now, they will not have the skills to step forward in the future. There is some limited evidence that the national focus on the minimal competencies called for under NCLB have played a role in our diminished attention to high-achieving students (Loveless, 2008). This research found that since the enactment of NCLB, low-achieving students have made solid progress while the gains of high-achieving students have been more modest.

In another study, Watkins and Sheng (2008) tracked the progress of advanced elementary students from third through eighth grade on Illinois' ISAT examination. They found the number of such students scoring in the "Exceeds" category in reading dropped as much as half between grades five and eight. On the other hand, others have stated we have never paid that much attention to our advanced learners, even before NCLB (Plucker, Burroughs, & Song, 2010). If attention can be equated with funding, there is little doubt fewer resources have been devoted to advanced learners than academically struggling students in most states. This does not bode well for the group from which the nation's future leaders are likely to be drawn.

The nation has its share of low-income advanced learners. Wyner, Bridgeland, and DiIulio (2009) have estimated 3.4 million advanced learners live in homes below the national median income level and over 1 million of these qualify for free or reduced lunch. They found these students are more likely to fall behind in achievement as time progresses and they are more likely than their peers from middle- and upper-income homes to drop out of high school. They are also less likely to enroll in college or earn a degree. In recent years, advanced learners have come to be known as "high flyers" in some circles.

While some of these high flyers continue to perform at high levels, the performance of 30 to 50 percent of these students declines (Xiang, Dahlin, Cronin, Theaker, & Durant, 2011) over time. The authors call these students with declining scores "descenders." While the percent of minority high flyers remained similar over time, the percent of high flyers from low-income homes declined. Also, high-achieving boys were most likely to become descenders. Clearly, not all students automatically overcome the impact of a lack of attention.

It is increasingly obvious that strictly focusing on minimum competency levels is unlikely to move students to the highest levels of achievement. The targets are simply not high enough. Antithetically, simply focusing on the highest levels of excellence for all is not likely to bring all students up to the level of competence. Just as trickle-down economics in a past decade did not spread the wealth to all; it is unwise to think that a similar approach with advanced learners will automatically pull up those other academically struggling students. However, there are strategies that can be more widely implemented to better meet the needs of our high flyers.

School principals and school district superintendents, working with their teachers and with the understanding and support of their boards of education, should step forward and take major accountability for the advanced learners in our schools. Administrators should expect teachers to employ differentiated instruction in their classrooms. This will take staff development and instructional support. Temporarily organizing students by ability levels for instruction, clustering advanced learners in specific classrooms, and encouraging teachers to receive specialized training to better enable them to work with advanced learners are all possible approaches. Advanced placement classes, honors classes, dual credit options, and International Baccalaureate programs are additional considerations at the high school level.

Nationally, the federal government could take more responsibility for funding work with advanced learners. This country spends many millions of dollars annually to support work with students on the lower end of the academic spectrum. Alternatively, most funding for students at the top end has been reduced or totally eliminated in recent years. It would also be useful if the federal government totally shifted to a growth model when addressing student progress. This has been permitted in a few states under NCLB waivers. Focusing upon growth rather than proficiency would be a positive step forward.

The other group being ignored, some would say being "written off," are those students far below the bubble. Some educators believe these students are so far behind they will never catch up with their peers. In an environment of limited time, scare resources, and increasing accountability demands, these students are given no additional assistance. What is to become of these children? What can their future be without a decent education?

Pauline Lipman studied two low-income African American Chicago schools and found they focused on centralized control and accountability. These schools were filled with children below the bubble. She stated, "The dispositions and identities produced by this sort of schooling prepare students for low-skill, low-paid jobs in the growing service economy"(Lipman, 2004, p. 103). These schools were but two of over five hundred elementary schools in Chicago. Clearly, some Chicago elementary schools are more successful than the two studied by Lipman. However, the accountability policies of the Chicago Public Schools were, and still are, to promote a narrow focus on high-stakes tests. Chicago is but one of thousands of school districts with this narrow accountability focus.

According to the currently prevalent definition of accountability, a school is only as good as its test scores. A good school is simply a high-scoring school. Ironically, if the test scores drop, or even fail to advance next year, then that school can become a bad school, even though all other aspects of the school remain the same. Under federal guidelines, the creativity embedded within a school is not considered for accountability purposes. The push to promote higher-order thinking skills does not matter as long as enough students are meeting the AYP challenge. The offering of elective courses, honors, and Advanced Placement courses and a wide range of student activities are of no consequence if students perform well enough on their state-mandated tests. Conversely, even though a school may boast of a state qualifying scholar bowl team or a regional Math Counts champion team, if it fails to meet AYP standards in even one area, it is judged a failure by state and federal officials.

THE NEXT GENERATION

Increasingly, students in educational administration programs have never known a professional world without NCLB. This is very true in principal preparation programs and is becoming more common among candidates for the superintendency. Those individuals who began their teaching careers after January 8, 2002, when NCLB was signed into law by President George W. Bush are now in their early to mid-thirties. These individuals see the current accountability system, driven by student test scores, as normal. Increasing numbers of states are attaching at least a portion of teacher evaluation to the performance of their students on state-mandated tests. The same is happening with principal evaluation in some states. As teachers, these individuals have continually received the message that the tested subjects and grade levels are more important and critical than the rest of the curricular scope and sequence.

While more experienced current administrators are aware of the significant increase of the role of the federal government in state and local educational decision making, the level of federal influence seems normal to younger educators. Even though the U.S. Constitution reserves education as a state function, and even though federal funding still constitutes less than 10 percent of the budget of most school districts, federal influence has become immense since the implementation of NCLB. Even though federal dollars may only constitute a fraction of the average school district's budget, in today's difficult economy, most districts are unable or unwilling to forgo those dollars. It should also be understood that the very poorest districts, with the largest percent of academically challenged students, receive a larger proportion of their funding through federal programs, such as Title I. With these dollars come regulations and a heavy federal stick to enforce those regulations.

Also unknown by many of today's administrative candidates is that the American public education system was once the envy of the world. The United States was praised for the creativity of its educators, and educators came to the United States from other countries to study our system at all levels. Much has often been made about the number of Nobel Prize winners produced by the U.S. public school system. Part of this American success story was the fact individuals in a wide range of fields were able to "think outside the box." They were never really constrained by a narrow curriculum focused upon tested items. While there were often state guidelines for school districts to follow such as minimal high school graduation requirements, school districts had a great deal of latitude regarding curricular decision making. While the subjects and courses offered were probably more similar than different, individual districts always had the flexibility to offer special courses and programs to meet local needs and demands.

Over the years, due to the U.S. reform movements previously mentioned, and by the implementation of NCLB, many school districts have lost this creativity. Districts are now being driven to become more similar than different. If examples are needed, consider how Response to Intervention (RtI) and the Common Core standards are being implemented in schools across the nation. While these initiatives have positive elements, these programs, along with the quest to make AYP, are driving school improvement and staff development efforts rather than the creativity of school teachers and administrators. This is particularly true of the school districts most dependent upon federal dollars; most commonly those with a high proportion of low-income students. Remember, the sanctions for failure under NCLB are much more severe for Title I schools and Title I schools educate substantial numbers of low-income students. Why do we have such a disparity in the percent of low-income students across our nation's schools?

FISCAL INEQUALITY

Because public education is a state function in the United States, the funding of public schools has been left primarily to the states and to the local school boards in most communities across the country. This has led to school funding formulas in most states which depend upon a combination of state-aid, local property tax revenue, and a small amount of federal funding. Many states employ a "foundation-level" approach to funding their schools. Through various means, the states determine a particular foundation level of funding is needed in order to provide an adequate education for the students in its public schools. In most states employing this method, the dollars actually come from all three sources, not just from state revenues. A major issue that has arisen since the economic downturn of 2008 is that some states are now determining adequacy of funding based upon fiscal realities rather than education rationale.

Because local property taxes play such an important role in educational funding, some districts are able to provide higher levels of educational opportunities for their students than other districts. The property tax portion of a school district's budget is generated by the overall taxable wealth of the district, often called the Equalized Assessed Valuation (EAV). A district with expensive homes or high levels of commercial activity will have a higher EAV than a district with little business and inexpensive homes. This disparity makes its way into the school funding formula in at least two ways. First, it takes a lower tax rate to generate funding for a district with a high EAV than in a district with a lower tax base. In other words, residents in a poorer district will probably face a higher tax rate than their peers in wealthier districts in order to provide the same level of funding.

Second, the residents of wealthier districts are often not happy with the same level of funding as their neighbors in poorer districts. They are willing and able to tax themselves at higher levels to provide what they see as a superior education for their children. Education aside, many residents in such districts see a correlation between the quality of the public schools and home values. Such individuals are willing and able to initially spend more for a home and subsequently pay more in taxes to protect these home values. This inequity exists in most states, to some degree.

This funding disparity can be significant. In Illinois, some districts spend three to four times as much per student as do others (Fritts, 2012). Several other states have a similar three-to-one ratio of disparity among districts. This means that those students being raised in families that have been able to give them many advantages also have access to better prepared teachers, better equipment and supplies, and wider curricular offerings. Such students are often educated in newer buildings with updated technology and in neighborhoods considered to be "safe." The advantages these students enjoyed upon entering school are thus perpetuated by the system.

There can also be disparities within school districts, based on residential housing patterns. While there would seem to be equity in terms of funding within particular districts, this may not always be the case. Due to negotiated agreements and district transfer rules, the better-prepared teachers may choose to transfer to the more affluent buildings at the first opportunity. Often, the older school facilities may be in the poorer sections of the district. These buildings often pose more challenges in terms of the ability to retrofit them for new technologies and modification of the space to house new programs, and they often lack adequate playground space. Voters in such districts may be reluctant to approve referenda to either construct new buildings in these neighborhoods or to vote for major renovations.

There have been numerous court challenges to the perceived inequity in school funding over the years. Using Illinois as an example, two cases are illustrative. The first was *Committee for Educational Rights v. Edgar* (1996). In this case, over sixty Illinois school districts joined together in a suit, claiming that the Illinois school funding formula was discriminatory for multiple reasons. At the trial court level, the plaintiffs claimed that since the system resulted in vast disparities in the level of funding and educational resources available to different districts based on property wealth, it was not "efficient" as related to the Illinois Constitution. The second claim at the trial court level was that under the funding scheme, funding is insufficient to provide a "high-quality" education to at-risk children.

The case was dismissed at the trial court level, so the plaintiffs brought the case before the appellate court, where they added another complaint to the original claims at the trial court level. They claimed that districts with low property bases are unable to provide a high-quality education to their students due to inadequate funding. Ultimately, the case made it to the Illinois Supreme Court where the high court dismissed the complaints brought forward in *Committee for Educational Rights v. Edgar*, but the decision was not unanimous. One justice agreed the plaintiffs had standing on the claim poorer districts were unable to provide a high-quality education to their at-risk children. The majority of justices in this case held that the disparity in funding between school districts was related to the legitimate state goal of promoting local control of education. The court also stated there were no judicially manageable standards to determine whether the state was providing a high quality of education as required by the Illinois Constitution.

The second noteworthy case that went to the Illinois Supreme Court was *Carr v. Koch*, which was decided in 2012. In this case, the primary plaintiffs were two educators, one from the south suburbs of Chicago and the other from Cairo, the southernmost community in Illinois. This suit took a different approach to the funding issue. The plaintiffs claimed the Illinois school funding formula had a disparate impact upon them as taxpayers. They claimed residents of poorer school districts were required to pay a proportionately higher property tax rate than their peers in wealthier districts and that their schools were still not comparable.

In their complaint, the plaintiffs cited numerous examples of these disparities. For example, they claimed taxpayers in property-poor Illinois K–8 school districts paid a median property tax rate that was 23 percent higher than similarly situated taxpayers in property rich K–8 districts. At the same time, the poorer districts received a median operating expense that was 28 percent lower than in property-rich districts. They also acknowledged a major finding of *Committee for Educational Rights v. Edgar*; that the disparity in state funding was related to the legitimate state goal of promoting local control of education. However, they argued that since the *Edgar* decision, individual schools and school districts in Illinois no longer exercised control over their schools, having abandoned local control to centralized decision making by the defendant, the Illinois State Board of Education (ISBE). The Illinois Supreme Court dismissed the plaintiffs' complaint, this time on a 7-0 vote. In Illinois, as in other states, the courts have been reluctant to criticize local property taxes as a major basis for state school funding mechanisms.

When facing accountability obligations to residents and students in districts with diverse housing patterns, administrators may face the dilemma of whether to support a neighborhood-school concept or a levels approach regarding district organizational structure. Clearly, many parents prefer the neighborhood-school concept for a variety of reasons. They may have purchased a home so that their children could attend a particular school. They may desire having their children attend a school close to home and with children from their neighborhood. Often, neighborhood elementary schools may be organized in a fashion that allows students to spend their entire elementary career in one building. Alternatively, neighborhood schools perpetuate any educational advantages or disadvantages arising from residential housing patterns.

An alternative to the neighborhood-school concept is when a district organizes schools by levels, and all children within particular age ranges attend the same school or series of leveled zone schools if the district is larger. For example, a district may send all children to the same primary school, and then to the same intermediate school, and so on. They may subsequently even attend the same middle school and high school. When all children from across a district attend the same school at particular grade levels, it does even out the playing field pertaining to teaching staff and resources. The disadvantages from the parental perspective may be longer bus routes for their children and more frequent moves among the leveled schools. In order to accommodate the number of children to be educated from throughout the district, each school may only accommodate two or three grade levels as opposed to five or six grades. Another issue with leveled schools, somewhat analogous to magnet schools, is that students' school friends may not live in the same neighborhoods and parents and guardians may find it more difficult to accommodate after-school playtimes and other activities.

Over the years, many central office administrators have dealt with the issue of neighborhood schools versus grade-level centers, and many more are likely to face the same dilemma in the future. To whom are administrators accountable in this situation? If they are to be accountable to parents, which group of parents should they favor? On one hand, some parents prefer the neighborhood-school concept and wish to keep their children close to home. On the other hand, another set of parents see the grade-level center concept as a means of achieving a degree of social justice for their children. This issue often splits members of a school district's board of education.

RESEGREGATION

When the *Brown v. Board of Education* decision was unanimously rendered by the U.S. Supreme Court in 1954, it was expected by many that schools across the nation would be integrated with "all deliberate speed," as called for in the Supreme Court's decision. However, the move toward integration took another two to three decades to accomplish, happening more quickly in some communities than others. Since housing was segregated in many parts of the United States, this made the integration of schools more of a logistical challenge. Often, this called for the busing of students out of their neighborhoods into other parts of the community for educational purposes. While this busing could go either way, either sending white students into minority neighborhoods, or vice versa, it was often the minority community that made concessions and agreed to have their children bused to the often more affluent, predominately white schools.

In some communities where resistance to school integration was strong, federal desegregation orders were put into place, essentially forcing these communities to integrate their schools. Under such orders, it was typical to mandate a minority enrollment in each school, which fell within a range that could not be more than 15 percent above or 15 percent below the overall percent of minority enrollment within the district. Achieving this type of balance led to a periodic redrawing of school zone attendance boundaries as well as decisions regarding busing students to help achieve this balance. These federal desegregation orders were met with continued resistance in some communities and with some degree of acceptance in others. Some communities faced the phenomenon of "white flight" or with the establishment of private schools and academies in order to avoid forced integration. Other communities were much more accepting, with some districts voluntarily racially balancing their schools, even without desegregation orders.

One such example was the St. Louis area, which engaged in a voluntary interdistrict program, beginning with five school districts in 1981. The City of St. Louis has its own school district, and the adjacent St. Louis County has multiple school districts. Then, as now, the St. Louis City Schools were predominately African American in enrollment. Over the years, this program expanded to include approximately a dozen county schools. At its peak, in the early 1990s, over thirteen thousand city students were bused out to county schools.

It should be noted this program also allowed county students to attend city magnet schools. During the early 1990s, up to eleven hundred students exercised this option. Over the years, this program has been renewed at least twice. Currently, the program is set to expire at the end of the 2013–2014 school year unless it is renewed by the transfer board. Presently, approximately fifty-two hundred students are participating in the program. In their study of this program, Wells and Crain (1997) found that "minority students who attended middle- and upper-class schools had higher educational achievement and college attendance rates than their peers in concentrated poverty schools."

Over the years, fewer federal desegregation orders were issued and others were allowed to expire. At the same time, housing patterns remained desegregated in many communities. In 2007, in *Parents Involved in Community Schools v. Seattle School District No. 1*, the U.S. Supreme Court ruled 5–4 against assigning students to public schools only for the purpose of achieving racial integration, and they also declined to recognize racial balancing as a compelling state interest. In an unusual twist to the case, Associate Justice Anthony Kennedy, one of the majority justices, was narrower in his interpretation. He said that while schools may use "race conscious" measures in the attempt to achieve diversity in schools, he felt that the schools in this case had been too broad in their plan. While this does not totally shut the door on the practice of modifying school boundaries or busing for the purposes of integration, it would take a very bold school district to challenge the *Parents Involved* decision.

What is the problem with segregated neighborhoods, and hence, segregated schools? Neighborhoods in the United States tend to be separated by income levels, and in many instances, to be minority may also mean one is poor. It is unlikely this pattern of segregated neighborhoods will be broken. The problem is not necessarily one of race, but of poverty. As already mentioned in this chapter, the more affluent school districts are able to provide a much more substantial funding base for their schools.

Many believe the opportunity gap among children from families of differing income levels is growing greatly. In a change from just a generation ago, college-educated parents now spend an hour more a day with their children than working-class parents. The wealthier parents also invest much more money in their children than do parents from low income levels—up to ten times more for tutoring and extracurricular types of activities. Forty years ago, students from the families in the bottom 25 percent of earners participated in student activities at approximately the same rate as students from wealthier families. Today, participation rates in extracurricular activities are worlds apart, with the poorer students being left far behind.

A VOICE OF EXPERIENCE

When the author was first a building principal, beginning in 1979, he learned that student academic performance was more an issue of income than race or ethnicity. He continues to hold that belief today. It is puzzling that more courts in various jurisdictions have not recognized the fact that the inequitable funding of our school districts leads to inferior educational opportunities for many students in disadvantaged neighborhoods. The author believes such rulings are political rather than educational in nature. He had the opportunity to travel to Finland in 2012 and interview Pasi Sahlberg about the Finnish educational system. Finland has a social welfare state that guarantees those students in the poorer areas are provided with the strongest education possible, thus leveling the playing field for students throughout the country. It is unlikely that the United States will shift to a similar system, with its concomitant tax rate of 40–50 percent.

However, the United States needs to recognize, as a nation, that it is ultimately cheaper and more ethical to properly educate low-income students at the beginning, rather than to send them to prison later. The U.S. public education has been a great contributor to the success of the nation but the public education system has lost some relevance. Many U.S. public schools are still producing students who compete very well on all of the major international assessments. Of course there are failing schools, but those schools are the exception and educators need to creatively address the needs of those schools. Specific strategies for addressing those issues are proposed in the last chapter of the book.

Another concern of the author, as a current professor of educational administration, is that the youngest administrative candidates have known nothing other than life under No Child Left Behind. When the author retired from the superintendency in 2005, one of his first research projects addressed this issue. As a superintendent near the end of his career, he sensed school districts were beginning to focus primarily on tested areas and this was having an impact on school improvement planning and staff development in an increasing number of school districts. A statewide survey of superintendents in 2006 confirmed this suspicion. School improvement planning and staff development were increasingly being directed toward improving mathematics, reading, and test-taking skills. The author is concerned that most recent graduates of administration programs do not fully appreciate the importance of the subjects beyond the tested areas.

SUMMARY

This chapter began with a brief overview of three national education reform movements that have transpired over the past three decades. The Excellence Movement, the Restructuring Movement, and the Standards Movement have all played a role in increasing the accountability faced by educational administrators. The Standards Movement is still active, and the most recent iteration of this movement calls for teachers, and in some cases, principals, to be held accountable for student scores on state-mandated tests. It is likely that this aspect of accountability will spread to additional states and that it will also soon be incorporated into the evaluation of district superintendents.

The group of students now known as the "bubble kids" was also discussed in the chapter. In many instances, educational accountability seems to have been reduced to how well students score on state-mandated tests. Accountability has become synonymous with making AYP on these tests in order to meet the requirements of NCLB. Since human and fiscal resources are scarce, many school districts have narrowed both their school improvement and staff development efforts to concentrate upon those students on the verge of either meeting or failing to meet AYP standards. A disproportionate amount of teacher and administrative time is spent working with these children, often to the detriment of those students at both the top and bottom of the academic achievement ladder.

The fact that many of today's teachers and administrators have known nothing other than the NCLB accountability system was discussed. Then, the chapter turned to an overview of the fiscal inequity that exists among the nation's public school systems. Since most states fund their schools with a combination of state revenue, federal funding, and local property taxes, some school districts are much more able than others to provide sufficient funding for their schools, based upon the property wealth of their districts. Thus, some districts, within the same state, may spend three to four times as much on their students than their poorer neighboring districts. In spite of numerous court challenges, this type of system remains in place in many states.

The chapter concluded with the assertion that the U.S. public schools are being resegregated, based upon the continuance of segregated housing patterns and the expiration or termination of federally mandated school desegregation orders. The 2007 U.S. Supreme Court decision in *Parents Involved in Community Schools v. Seattle District No. 1* made it very unlikely that forced desegregation of public schools will be used in the foreseeable future to integrate schools. It was also contended that academic differences among students are more likely related to low income and lack of opportunities rather than to racial differences; although in America, to be minority often means that one is also poor.

TWO
Why Money Matters

In the first chapter of this book, it was asserted school districts are inequitably funded within states, and among the states. Why should this matter? Many states utilize a "foundation-level" formula approach to education, which often combines state dollars, federal funds, and local property tax revenues to provide a foundation level of funding that is supposed to provide an adequate level of funding, and hence, an adequate education, to students in each district. There are several problems with this theory and the first among these is that the structure of most of these systems ensures the districts with the wealthiest families also provide higher per capita levels of educational funding for their children than do the poorer districts. Education has proven to be beneficial to most of the taxpayers of the wealthier school districts, and they are willing to pay higher taxes to guarantee their children receive the best educational benefits possible. Thus, the children who have received the benefits of a comfortable lifestyle, such as trips, reading materials, and educational games, subsequently attend schools with the best teachers and educational equipment possible.

Another fallacy of our current system is that the "foundation level" is actually adequate. Historically, in most parts of the country, the states' contributions to these foundation levels increased steadily until the financial crisis hit in 2008, but since that time, the states' levels of contributions to the foundation level have flattened out in some cases, and have actually decreased in other situations. In at least one state, the legislature and state board of education have maintained that the foundation level has remained the same but payments into this foundation level have been prorated at substantially less than 100 percent for multiple years. Whether the educational program was ever adequate in those districts relying upon the minimal foundation is questionable. This becomes almost a moot point after the elimination of thousands of teaching positions across the country since the financial crisis began. While both poorer and wealthier districts have faced these financial challenges, many of the wealthier districts began with financial reserves that have helped them weather the storm.

EDUCATION DEBT

One of the most common terms used in public education over the past several years has been the "achievement gap." We know academic achievement levels differ greatly between white and minority students in many locations; particularly in those situations where race and income are linked. One of the contributing considerations in the passage of the NCLB Act was the achievement gap between white and minority students. Among other things, NCLB has led to the division of students into subgroups, so minority achievement can no longer be masked, either intentionally or unintentionally in the reporting of test results. Many of our school improvement and staff development efforts today are focused upon reducing the achievement gap in our schools. One of the goals of measuring AYP is the hope of erasing the achievement gap by having 100 percent of all students meet AYP which would theoretically ensure the academic achievement of students would be comparable.

Gloria Ladson-Billings (2006) has introduced the concept of the education debt in which she compares the achievement gap to the federal budget deficit, but then matches what she calls the education debt to the national debt. Eliminating the achievement gap or managing the federal budget without a deficit would both be positive events, but in either case we would still be left with either an educational debt, or a national debt, both of which have negative consequences. Failing to address our national debt leads to the necessity of making interest payments on that debt. In 2012, the interest on the U.S. national debt was projected to be $220 billion, which was fourth in governmental expenditures behind the Department of Defense, Medicare, and Medicaid (Kurtzleben, 2012). Just think where our schools might be today if even a portion of those interest payments over the years had been diverted to support public education, or even more specifically, to assist struggling schools and school districts.

Just as it has taken centuries for us to accumulate our present level of national debt, the same is true for our educational debt. Educational inequalities in this country were historically based upon race, class, and gender. Initially, it was often felt girls did not need to be educated, or at least not to the same level as boys. In some states, many of the early schools were either private schools or subscription schools, and the tuition was out of reach for many families. However, the most pervasive inequality in the U.S. public education system has been based on race.

Prior to the U.S. Civil War, it was illegal to educate African Americans in several states. While the outcome of the Civil War ended this practice, this did not lead to equality of educational opportunity for blacks. After the period of post–Civil War Reconstruction, the United States slipped into an era of "separate but equal," which was reinforced and codified by the 1896 U.S. Supreme Court decision, *Plessy v. Ferguson*. While this was initially a case about the right to ride a particular street car in New Orleans, it also came to have widespread implications for education. It did not take long for the impact of this ruling to permeate American society.

While segregated schools were not totally universal throughout the United States, they were very common in both the Southern and Northern states. Missouri, which was a border state during the Civil War, is an interesting example of "separate but equal." Immediately after the Civil War, the 1865 Missouri Constitution stated that schools for African Americans were permissible and by 1875, they were mandatory, but they were to be separate from white schools and only needed to be established if the number of eligible African American students in a community reached a particular threshold number. Even more onerous was the fact that if the average daily attendance fell below a particular minimum number in any one month, the school had to be closed for up to six months (Morice and Hunt, 2008). This led to a pattern of frequent school openings and closings in various counties throughout the state where the African American population was sparse. Of course, these threshold numbers applied only to the "colored" schools.

There were instances in which teachers and school directors were willing to educate black and white children together. One such case was in Grundy County, Missouri, which is located in the northern portion of the state. In the late 1880s, an African American farmer named William Brummell had four school-aged children, but there was no established school for African American school children within his home school district. Since his children were the only African American children of school age within the district the closest school that his children were eligible to attend was in the County Seat of Trenton, three and one-half miles away. The white teacher and the three white school directors of the local school gave William Brummell permission for his children to attend the school in his neighborhood.

However, a group of five white parents objected to the education of the Brummell children in the neighborhood school and took the matter to court. Eventually, the case made its way to the Missouri Supreme Court, which ruled in 1890, in *Lehew v. Brummell*, that it was illegal for white and black students to be educated together (Hunt and Morice, 2008). This ruling essentially solidified "separate but equal" schools in Missouri until after the *Brown v. Board* U.S. Supreme Court ruling in 1954. It eliminated the possibility of white and black children being educated together. This provision was not stricken from the Missouri statutes until 1957.

Native American students were also subjected to an inferior education. Many Native American children were sent to mission schools or to boarding schools. The purpose of both types of schools was to convert the children to Christianity and, some say, to provide a cheap labor source for the church. Another purpose of these schools was to stamp out the native culture and to force the assimilation of these children into the white way of life. Few colleges and universities accepted these students, and those that were able to enter higher education often were channeled into vocational tracks.

Latina/o students were also subjected to discrimination and segregation in terms of their educational opportunities. Like African American students, Latina/o students were often educated in inferior facilities, with secondhand textbooks and, in some cases, less than stellar teachers. The first major case that impacted Latina/o students was a case coming out of Orange County, California, *Mendez v. Westminster* (1946). In this case, a group of five fathers successfully sued, stating that their children faced discrimination by being assigned to "Mexican" schools within the school district. The fathers won at the district court level, but the school district appealed the case to the Ninth Federal District Appellate Court in San Francisco.

The appellate court upheld the lower court decision, ruling in favor of the parents. In a precursor to the *Brown v. Board* (1954) decision, Governor Earl Warren then signed into law the repeal of remaining segregationist provisions of the California statutes. It is also significant that the NAACP filed an *amicus curiae* brief on behalf of the plaintiffs, and the NAACP was represented in this action by Thurgood Marshall. In 1954, both Warren and Marshall played major roles in the *Brown* case. California was not the only state that had issues with the education of Latina/o youth.

Another case advancing the cause of Latina/o students was decided in Texas in 1954, and although not an educational rights case, *Hernandez v. Texas* (1954) did have a major impact upon the schools of Texas. This case involved the jury selection in a murder case in Jackson County, Texas. In Texas, Mexican Americans were not technically considered to be minorities, but they were certainly treated in a discriminatory manner in all phases of life, including schooling. Although Jackson County had a sizable Mexican American population in the 1950s, no Mexican American had been selected to serve on a jury in twenty-five years. In this case, which advanced to the U.S. Supreme Court in 1954, the state of Texas argued that Mexican Americans were not considered to be minorities, thus they had not been discriminated against. The U.S. Supreme Court disagreed, and ruled that the Fourteenth Amendment protects those beyond the racial classes of white and black and extended to other racial groups, including Mexican Americans.

Does the education debt still exist? Some would argue that while discrimination occurred in the past, the lingering results of that discrimination should surely have been ameliorated by this point in time. How long does it take to wipe the slate clean of past injustices? Are there still residual effects of past practices and if so, how long will it be before all students are able to enter the educational arena on equal footing? In a powerful address delivered at the commencement ceremony at Howard University on June 4, 1965, President Lyndon B. Johnson talked about taking an individual who had been bound in chains, liberating him and directing him to the starting line and expecting that he would be able to run a race on an equal footing.

Then, President Johnson said:

> To this end equal opportunity is essential, but not enough, not enough. Men and women of all races are born with the same range of abilities. But ability is not just the product of birth. Ability is stretched or stunted by the family that you live with, and the neighborhood that you live in—by the school you go to and the poverty or richness of your surroundings. It is the product of a hundred unforeseen forces playing upon the little infant, the child, and finally the man. (Johnson, 1965)

Related to this, Wolfe and Haveman (2001) talk about the nonmarket and intergenerational effects of schooling, citing a positive link between an individual's own education and the education received by that person's children. There are also links between education and the health status of individuals and their families. The quality of consumer choices made by individuals can also be tied to the educational level attained as well as fertility choices and the level of criminal activity. The relationship between level of education and earning power of individuals is well known, and while the earnings ratio gap among various racial and ethnic subgroups may have narrowed over the years, the cumulative impact of income disparities still influences the efficacy of minorities in areas such as involvement in school activities such as leadership in parent-teacher organizations, booster clubs, and school boards. Indeed, many communities that have not been the beneficiaries of a good educational system have a suspicion and distrust of their public schools and what the school system can do for them and their families. Whose responsibility is it to determine the level of education debt that still exists in our public schools, and more important, who should be accountable for addressing this situation?

SEPARATE BUT EQUAL?

If skin color was the only difference between predominately white schools and those schools comprised primarily of minority students, then segregated schools could conceivably be equal. Indeed, there are examples of schools with large minority populations that claim to provide their students with an excellent education. However, these schools are the exception rather than the rule and even some of these fail to hold up to scrutiny, according to one author. Richard Rothstein (2004) says that claims regarding the Heritage Foundation's "no excuses" schools, the Education Trust's "high-flying" schools, and even Douglas Reeves' "90/90/90" schools cannot substantiate all of their claims of student success under close examination. While he does not dispute that some of the schools cited by these groups and by Dr. Reeves may indeed exhibit substantial levels of success, Rothstein claims that often the data utilized apply only to particular grade levels or subjects and that in other cases, the schools are not "typical" low-income schools, although they may be largely populated by low-income families. Some of the schools cited were magnet or choice schools, which required an active interest and/or choice on the part of parents regarding student enrollment and participation.

Rothstein expands on the value of parental involvement, including low-income parents, saying, "Schools to which low-income parents apply almost certainly have a disproportionate share of unusually able children. Parents who go to the effort to apply to a particular school are more likely to provide literacy support at home and to monitor children's school efforts" (2004, p. 72). While it is not logical to assume that all low-income families have the same dedication to or understanding of the value of education, many children from low-income families also live in inadequate housing and do not have access to quality health care. Their parents may be poorly educated and there may also be high levels of family stress. When considering minority poor children, their family struggles with income may go back generations, as opposed to some poor white families, in which their financial woes may be more episodic. There will always be some poor minority children who will have higher academic achievement levels than poor or even middle-class white children, but how to raise the achievement level of all low-income children is a complex issue.

The evidence is indisputable that the United States is returning to segregated schools. In 2005 Orfield and Lee (p. 5) stated, "U.S. schools are now 41 percent nonwhite and the great majority of the nonwhite students attend schools which now show substantial segregation." There is a strong link between minority status and income level in this country, and the data have consistently shown that lower-income children do not typically perform as well as their higher-income peers on standardized achievement tests. Still, many people, including legislators, believe that separate schools can become equal and that our nation's abandonment of the concept of integrated schools is not a major issue. What these individuals ignore is the evidence going back as far as the Coleman Report (Coleman et al., 1966), which was the first large national study of both segregated and desegregated schools. This report found that only family background had a stronger influence on educational achievement than peer influence.

Several research studies have shown attending a middle-class school exposes lower-income minority students to higher educational expectations and to a broader range of life options (Schofield in Banks, 2004; Dawkins & Braddock, 1994; Anyon, 1997; and Natriello, McDill, & Pallas, 1990) Since the middle-class schools in this country are becoming increasingly white, or more segregated, what does this say about the chances for poor minority students to have the opportunity for peer interaction with more affluent students? If students spend their entire childhood in low-income segregated neighborhoods, where education may not be generally valued, and subsequently attend segregated schools in those same neighborhoods, how will they ever know what possibilities exist beyond the boundaries of their daily lives? The schools in poor neighborhoods are more likely to be housed in old and inadequate facilities. The supplies, materials, and instructional technology available are all likely to lag behind what is generally available in middle-income schools.

It is possible all of this could be overcome by excellent, well-trained and energetic teachers. However, the greatest gap between low-income and middle-income schools may be teacher quality. High-poverty schools have difficulty attracting and retaining high-quality teachers. According to one study by Linda Darling-Hammond (2003), California schools with highly concentrated minority enrollments were less likely to have properly certified mathematics and science teachers. Other studies have shown there tends to be higher teacher turnover in high-minority and high-poverty schools.

There are rare examples of excellent, dedicated teachers willing to devote their careers working with disadvantaged youth in low-income school settings. However, the more typical setting in American public education is for new teachers to gain initial experience working in either less affluent schools or in lower-level classes, and then moving out or upward over time. Many of those starting in low-income schools move into middle- or upper-income settings, and those beginning with the basic subjects usually aspire to teach honors and advanced placement courses as they gain experience. Another recent phenomenon impacting this situation has been the national fiscal crisis, which has led to the elimination of thousands of teaching positions on a national level. Due principally to union contracts, the first teachers cut in such situations are the least experienced educators. This is not to imply that all new teachers are the strongest teachers, but they do often bring new ideas and a high energy level to a school and to the classroom.

Is a teacher a teacher? In other words, are all teachers essentially equal? The structure of most negotiated contracts between teachers' unions and their employers are based on the premise that teachers with the same levels of education and experience are equal and many contracts have historically included transfer clauses that give bidding preference to those teachers with the most seniority within the district. Antithetically, many contracts also set a limit on the involuntary transfer of teachers, with the implication being any teacher can fill any opening in any school, regardless of the nature of that school. With the passage of NCLB, the issue of highly qualified teachers came to the forefront, and the concept of highly qualified teachers seemed to imply that not all teachers are equal. A major intent of this portion of NCLB was to ensure that teachers were strongly prepared in their content areas and situations such that the previously cited California example of less-than-qualified mathematics and science teachers could be avoided.

Like many of the provisions of NCLB, the definition of what constitutes a highly qualified teacher was left to the individual states. Generally, there was a push to ensure or move toward substantial subject matter expertise among teachers. This caused varying degrees of consternation from state to state, with a number of states struggling with special education and middle-level certification issues, in particular. While it initially appeared that the highly qualified teacher provision might lead some teachers to advance their subject matter competence, how much of this actually happened is questionable. Many teachers were able to avoid additional training due to a provision of NCLB entitled High Objective Uniform State Standard of Evaluation (HOUSSE). Essentially, HOUSSE grandfathered thousands of teachers into compliance regarding subject matter background.

Another area where schools serving low-income areas may not be equal is the curricular offerings they provide to their students. A related issue in these schools is the expectation level often associated with the diminished curriculum that is offered. The curriculum gap between low-income and middle-income and upper-income schools begins in the primary grades. In one study pertaining to primary reading, Teale, Paciga, & Hoffman (2007) found low-income urban schools need more systematic and sustained instruction in comprehension, content knowledge, and writing in the early grades as well as emphasis on phonological awareness, decoding, word recognition, and reading fluency. These are areas often taken for granted by teachers in schools serving middle-class children.

We also hear of the dearth of minority students in advanced mathematics classes at the secondary level. One major problem is too many minority students, particularly African Americans, do not make it past algebra at the high school level. Many low-income high schools do not even offer the same high-level mathematics courses available to students in suburban schools and, of course, the precursor to the courses offered in high school begins at the middle school or junior high level. It is not at all uncommon for middle-level schools serving more affluent youth to have substantial numbers of students enrolled in algebra with even a portion of these students matriculating into geometry. Such middle school options enable students to move into courses such as calculus and discrete mathematics in high school. Contrast this with the general mathematics courses often taken by low-income youth.

Regardless of the level of coursework taken, the expectation level of teachers and administrators is of supreme importance. Unfortunately, both the teacher expectations and the curriculum offered in poverty schools often falls short. Kati Haycock, president of the Education Trust shared the following comments made by students in high-poverty schools:

> They talk about teachers who often do not know the subjects that they are teaching. They talk about counselors who consistently underestimate their potential and place them in lower-level courses. They talk about principals who dismiss their concerns. And they talk about a curriculum and a set of expectations that feel so miserably low-level that they literally bore the students right out the school door. (Haycock, 2001, pp. 7–8)

Haycock also stated her researchers from the Education Trust were "stunned" by how little is expected of students in high-poverty schools. Students in many of these schools are given very few assignments to complete on a daily or even weekly basis. The quality of those assignments that are given are marginal. The cumulative impact of this lack of rigor has now led to more than one generation of students ill-prepared to meet the demands of today's workforce environment. This is a terrible waste of lives and resources.

Regarding the availability of an equitable education, including good teachers, Linda Darling-Hammond (2006, p. 13) has stated that the ability to "develop both individual competence and a democratic community has been a myth rather than a reality for many Americans." She has perhaps done as much research as anyone on the conditions faced in poverty schools and has found them falling short in terms of class sizes, facilities, equipment, and qualified teachers. She says that most urban schools are now "majority minority" (2006, p. 14) and are funded at a much lower level than their suburban counterparts. The societal implications of this situation are enormous. The dropout problem in this nation is concentrated in our segregated high-poverty schools.

Half of the nation's African American and Latina/o students are dropping out (Orfield & Lee, 2005, p. 6). There was a time in this country when a high school dropout could still find a blue collar job and support a family, but those days are gone. The U.S. economy can no longer support unskilled workers, at least not as many as now exist. This situation has led to increases in welfare and crime; the school-to-prison pipeline is not just an urban legend in many communities. This should not be surprising in view of the national situation, which has us spending more on incarceration rather than education. In the decades of the 1980s and

1990s, three times as many African American men entered prison as entered college (Justice Policy Institute, 2002).

The United States stands alone among "advanced" nations in the size of its dropout rate. Most Asian and European nations now graduate 95 percent of their students, while the U.S. average has hovered between 75 and 80 percent. Finland is one example of the 95 percent graduation rate. While we would be thrilled in the United States with only a 5 percent high school dropout rate, Pasi Sahlberg, the author of *Finnish Lessons: What Can the World Learn from Educational Change in Finland?* (2010), estimates that every dropout will ultimately cost the Finnish economy 1 million euros over his/her lifetime (personal communication, Pasi Sahlberg, August 7, 2012). Just think of the financial impact of the dropout problem for the U.S. economy. It has been estimated that if we could cut our dropout rate in half, adding 700,000 additional high school graduates a year, this would provide a $90 billion annual boost to our economy (Levin & Rouse, 2012). This does not include the savings in prison costs, nor does it even address the societal and moral advantages of turning around this situation.

EXCELLENT TEACHERS ARE ESSENTIAL

We know many elements influence the quality of a school. Students must be educated in a safe and secure environment. It helps if the climate of the physical environment can be controlled and kept within comfortable ranges, and the lighting must be adequate. Students need to have access to current instructional materials and the availability of current technology can certainly help the situation. Instruction may be facilitated if class sizes are kept within reasonable ranges, particularly at the primary level. However, the existence of these items, or the lack of some of these items, can be impacted by the quality of the teacher in the classroom. An excellent teacher can help overcome deficits in the educational environment, while a poor teacher can squander the resources that may be available.

Earlier, the issue of whether a teacher is a teacher was raised, and it was asserted that many negotiated agreements assume that teachers are interchangeable. The implication is that as long as they hold the proper certification, they can do the job in any position for which they are endorsed. While initial certification may be a necessary condition for entering the profession, is it sufficient to ensure that teachers will have the knowledge and skills to face the challenges they are likely to encounter? Are all teacher preparation programs the same, or are some superior to others? Can teachers prepared in cookie-cutter education programs work equally well with all types of students, and what about those teachers prepared in alternative programs, such as Teach for America? How effective are those individuals without the proper certification, teaching on provisional certificates?

First, completing a sound teacher education program with a strong student teaching component does make a difference regarding how successful a new teacher is likely to be in the classroom. Darling-Hammond found in a South Carolina study (Darling-Hammond, 2003) that 64 percent of the total variance in student outcomes could be attributed to teacher qualifications. Anyone who has ever taught knows how difficult it can be, even with the benefit of a sound teacher education program. One day, you are a student teacher and the next day, you are the teacher. Not only do teachers need a strong background in their curriculum content areas, but also in pedagogical strategies and child development. Also essential is a wide range of pre-clinical experiences with actual students, capped off with an extended student teaching or internship experience.

Finland is a country valuing the extended internship period. Not only do teacher candidates receive extensive instruction in how to teach, with a strong focus on research incorporating best practices, but they also spend at least a year in a university model school, working directly with students. During this time, teacher candidates advance from basic practice, through advanced practice, and ultimately to final practice (Sahlberg, 2011, p. 36). The U.S. once had many university model or laboratory schools. Many universities, particularly those which began as normal schools, hosted university laboratory schools where teacher education candidates could work with students and hone their craft.

Over the years, most U.S. university laboratory schools have closed. In some cases, critics within the universities claimed that their university schools' populations were not representative of the community population, and that the children of university employees were overrepresented in enrollments. In other instances, university administrators saw the salary lines represented by the laboratory school teachers and chose to use those dollars for other priorities. Still other university leaders they felt they needed the space for regular university classes.

When new teachers enter the classroom either unprepared or ill-prepared and are forced to face the reality of the situation, it is a real wake-up call. Some of these teachers turn to their colleagues, their administrators, or other sources for help. Some districts assign an experienced mentor teacher to beginning educators and in other cases an experienced teacher will take a new teacher under his or her wing. There are also school districts that provide an induction program for new teachers. Unfortunately, with the economic climate that has engulfed the country since 2008, formal mentoring and induction programs are becoming increasingly scarce. Even with the assistance of a mentor, poorly prepared teachers may still struggle in the classroom.

Often, struggling new teachers will develop a teaching style that enhances their ability to control the classroom. Strategies such as the use of worksheets and other rote assignments, reading from the book, or the assignment of computer games and exercises without pedagogical purposes may become the norm. Such teachers are afraid to allow students to become engaged in active or creative activities. These teachers do not have enough tools in their kit bags to intellectually challenge students, particularly those coming from backgrounds different from their own. Unless these educators receive assistance and additional training, they typically become increasingly disenchanted with the teaching profession.

Either these teachers stay, doing a disservice to their students, or they leave the profession, contributing to the high mobility rate among teachers; particularly in high-poverty schools. Even though up to 50 percent of teachers leave the profession within the first five years of employment (Lambert, 2006), some poor teachers remain in the profession. Teachers are often conservative individuals, and may have entered the profession thinking that it would provide them with a stable income and guaranteed retirement plan. Many teachers simply find it difficult to consider moving to another field of work. Contrast the 50 percent attrition rate among American teachers with the 15 to 20 percent of Finnish teachers who leave the profession over their careers.

Regardless of the measures of teacher quality used, the least qualified teachers are found in disproportionate numbers in schools educating low-income and minority children. Whether one reviews the certification status, the quality of the teacher education program attended, the teachers' grades, or their years of experience, the teachers serving poor and minority youth fall short of those serving more advantaged students in this country. Those teachers with potential have a tendency to develop their skills in low-income schools and then move to more affluent settings. Overall, regardless of teacher quality, the attrition rate of teachers in such schools is much larger than in wealthier settings. This is a situation in need of resolution.

Much has been said in recent years about alternative certification and teacher preparation programs such as Teach for America. This program takes the best and brightest students from some of the nation's most prestigious universities and after a few weeks of training, places them in high-poverty classrooms. One major study found that certified teachers were typically more effective than noncertified teachers, including Teach for America students (Darling-Hammond & Bransford, 2005). When and if Teach for America graduates became certified after two or three years, they became as effective as other certificated teachers. However, nearly all Teach for America graduates left teaching after three years. One could say that disadvantaged youth may have benefited from the presence of Teach for America graduates in their classrooms, albeit for a short period of time. However, this has not proven to be a permanent situation and has done nothing to reduce the teacher mobility experience of low-income students.

Good teachers do matter. Multiple studies have shown a direct link between teacher quality and student achievement (Strauss & Sawyer, 1986; Darling-Hammond & Bransford, 2005). In one case, each 1 percent increase in teacher quality as indicated by National Teacher Examination scores brought about a corresponding 5 percent decline in failure rates by students on standardized competency examinations. Another study showed having an uncertified teacher in the classroom could reduce a student's achievement by three months over a year. Multiple uncertified teachers over an elementary school career could put a student a year or more behind, academically. Study after study has shown the very schools that most need high-quality teachers with little turnover have neither.

Who has accountability for the placement of poorly prepared teachers in low-income schools? This particular category of accountability has several layers. In many states, the legislature has fallen short of its responsibility to adequately fund the public schools within the state. Over the past two decades, many legislatures and governors have wrested control of the public schools away from the professional educators within their states, including the leaders of the state boards of education. Legislators and other governmental leaders have listened to the critics of public education, those stating that the entire public education system is broken.

Many governmental leaders have bought into the model of accountability that reduces quality to how well students score on standardized tests. At the same time, decision makers at the state level have heeded the calls for vouchers, charter schools, and outright privatization of schools. While some of these approaches may have merit, particularly well-run charters, in many cases they are merely ways of reducing the state's responsibility for the public schools. Legislators are also more prone to listen to constituents with money, power, and influence. Such individuals will do whatever it takes to ensure excellent educational results for their own children. The residents of the high-poverty school districts addressed in this chapter seldom have their voices heard by politicians.

Another layer of accountability for the employment of poor teachers rests with the major teacher unions of this country. Historically, both the American Federation of Teachers (AFT) and the National Education Association (NEA) have been primarily concerned with protecting their members. While the union leadership at the national, state, and regional levels all assert that they are interested in students, their first interest is their membership. This has led to the previously discussed situation in which unions consider teachers to be equal, regardless of their skills. Only seniority makes some teachers more equal than others. This mentality has manifested itself in such phenomena as standard salary schedules, seniority lists, transfer policies, and so on.

While a few union affiliates have experimented with approaches such as merit pay, such deviations from the norm have been the exception. Clearly, some states have a stronger union presence than others. Many former industrial states with a strong labor union background have also been hospitable to the unionization of teachers. Other states with more of a "right to work" tendency have been more open and flexible regarding teacher pay and work conditions. Colorado, for example, is one state that has experimented with differentiated pay schemes for teachers and has a robust charter school environment. Colorado became an open enrollment state in 1991 and did away with teacher tenure later in the 1990s.

Local boards of education have also influenced the quality of teachers employed within their school districts. Most boards are now facing major fiscal concerns, but even before the current fiscal crisis, some boards had a tendency to keep their salary schedules as low as possible, which was often couched in terms of being responsible to the taxpayers of the district. Some boards of education instructed or influenced their administrators to employ primarily beginning teachers with only a bachelor's degree. Rather than employing the best teacher for the job, some districts have routinely hired the least expensive teachers and many of these same districts have not encouraged teachers to pursue advanced training and graduate degrees. This lack of support often becomes part of the district culture and often manifests itself in the district's salary schedule in the form of fewer salary lanes and less reward for advanced education. In some cases, teachers have been hesitant to pursue advanced degrees until after receiving tenure in such districts.

Another influence some school boards have on the quality of the teaching staff in their districts is their tendency to hire primarily, and in some cases nearly exclusively, local residents as teachers and administrators. Naturally, some local residents prove to be excellent teachers. However, bringing in teachers from the outside can be a way of importing new ideas and diversity. Hiring outside candidates increases the probability of exposing local students to a wider range of ideas and techniques that may be engendered by teachers attending an expanded pool of universities and teacher preparation programs. In some urban areas, boards see the employment of local citizens as a way of boosting the local economy.

Superintendents also play a key role in the decisions made pertaining to the employment of teachers to staff their districts. Strong superintendents can influence boards of education to occasionally employ a more highly qualified teacher, even though that individual may be more expensive. These same superintendents can also encourage their boards to more frequently take a chance on outside candidates. This superintendent advocacy is particularly critical in the employment of minority teachers or in decisions to employ teachers with the training and skills to work with low-income youth. Once the new teachers with the requisite skills have been employed to join the district, superintendents can and do work tirelessly to make these new individuals feel welcome and accepted within the district and the community.

In a like manner, superintendents must facilitate staff development activities targeting strategies and techniques to make teachers more effective in educating low-income youth. Superintendents can take the lead in finding the funding and arranging the staff development activities. The superintendent must convince the board of education that such activities are critical to the well-being of the school district. Perhaps most importantly, the superintendent must "walk the talk" and show the entire professional staff this is a critical staff development activity. Just arranging it is not enough; the superintendent must also be an active participant. The superintendent must also commit to a long-term process in this regard.

Principals also play a key role in employing effective teachers for their buildings, manifesting leadership in many ways. First, principals must work to convince staff that employing new teachers with specialized skills for working with low-income youth is important. In some districts, the hiring recommendation may be left entirely to the principal, and in other situations, a teacher interview committee may be involved. The principal may be constrained by the provisions of a negotiated agreement where current district staff have first right of refusal for positions within the district. It may also be the principal's job to convince the superintendent and/or the board of education that the district needs to go in a different direction in its hiring practices. Regardless of the situation and circumstances, principals must use moral suasion to influence the hiring process and to ensure that the best candidates for each position are fairly considered and ultimately employed.

A VOICE OF EXPERIENCE

When the author was a superintendent he often told teachers and administrators that students were almost always capable of being pushed or challenged to a much higher degree than usually happened. He learned this during his first year of teaching, beginning in 1971 when he was one of four sixth-grade teachers in the school. The school departmentalized for mathematics and language arts, and the author was assigned the "low" mathematics group his first year, but it was not until well into the year that he discovered that his expectations for this group were much too low. Fortunately, he worked with three other very excellent and experienced teachers and a conversation with two of them one day put him on the right track with his students. The author sincerely believes that students can be academically challenged without increasing their levels of stress to unbearable levels. As long as higher expectations are presented as positive challenges and are accompanied with sufficient support from the teacher, expectation levels can be increased.

Another thing learned during that first year of teaching was that the schools in the community in which he taught had only become completely integrated in 1969, fully fifteen years after the *Brown v. Board* decision. This was a university community in Illinois. His eyes were opened when some of the materials that had been used in the Crispus Attucks School previously attended by the black students in the community were sent to his building for storage. He was stunned by how old and out of date the materials were that he examined. While progress has been made on the education debt outlined by Gloria Ladson-Billings, it has not been eliminated.

The other thing he learned over the years is that there can be an immense difference in the quality of teachers in any building or school district. While the vast majority of teachers with whom the author worked were very competent, some were at least a cut above the others. It was a joy to watch those individuals teach and when the author was having a bad day as a principal or superintendent, he would often drop in to a master teacher's room and watch that individual teach for a few minutes, inevitably leaving the room with an improved disposition. Conversely, each building or district is likely to have at least a few stinkers within the ranks. These are the teachers you would not want your own children subjected to for a year, or even a day. At the secondary level, students often self-select and are able to avoid such teachers. At the elementary level, placement of students with these teachers is not so easy, and principals are often left with the unenviable task of making potentially life-altering choices for students.

SUMMARY

This chapter addressed the concept that money matters to the education provided to public school students across the United States. The myth that the "foundation-level" funding method that is employed by many states actually provides equitable funding to all students was also addressed. Some wealthier communities have been willing to tax themselves at higher levels to provide more educational advantages for the children of those communities. As long as so many states rely on the local property tax as a substantial proportion of their foundation-level calculations, some students will be winners and others will be losers under this scenario. School equity court case results have been mixed to this point.

The concept of this nation's education debt, as outlined by Gloria Ladson-Billings, was discussed. While much of the attention of educational researchers and the press has been devoted to the achievement gap in the United States, the education debt also exists as a backlog of issues brought about by past educational practices in this country. Multiple historical examples were given of how the education debt accumulated in the United States and the rationale for its continued existence was advanced. This debt has disparately impacted low-income students and students from specific ethnic groups, which are often one and the same. Until the nation determines it is willing to reduce and ultimately eliminate the education debt, we will continue to have a two-tier society.

The concept of separate but equal schools was reviewed. Contrary to popular belief, schools segregated by race still exist in this country; indeed, their numbers are increasing. If the only issue of separate schools happened to be skin color, this might not have a major educational impact. However, to be minority in the United States more often than not also translates into being poor. Essentially, the country is now involved in the phenomenon of resegregation of its public schools. The schools serving the students living in highest poverty are the most poorly funded, often with substandard curricular materials and supplies and, almost inevitably, the weakest teachers.

The chapter concluded with a discussion of how and why the least prepared teachers tend to work in the low-income and high-minority schools. The fact that too few teachers are professionally prepared to work in such schools was addressed and the abysmal turnover rate of teachers in these schools was also considered. Alternative approaches to teacher preparation were mentioned. It was asserted that teacher quality does matter in terms of student academic achievement. Accountability for this failure to properly staff high-poverty schools was attributed to several categories and levels of individuals.

THREE
The Shadow System

Historically, the United States evolved with coexisting systems of public and private education. While the private schools were often religious in orientation, not all were. The vast majority of Americans attended and supported the public schools. Indeed, even the private school families supported the public schools through their property taxes. One of the hallmarks of our democracy has traditionally been our strong public school system.

For forty-four years, Phi Delta Kappa has commissioned a Gallup survey of Americans' attitudes toward public education. Year after year, respondents expressed satisfaction and confidence in their own public schools in particular. The more familiar people were with their schools, the happier they seemed to be with those institutions. Until the publication of *A Nation at Risk* (National Commission on Excellence in Education, 1983), Americans expressed confidence in their public schools. Even the challenge of Sputnik in 1957 did not quash national confidence in the public schools. Rather, it was determined that schools needed to redouble their efforts to keep the United States competitive. One of the major elements of that program was to train more high school mathematics and science teachers.

After the publication of *A Nation at Risk*, it became fashionable to criticize public education; some of this criticism was done openly and some was conducted more covertly. One of the first proposed suggestions to improve the public schools was to run the schools more like businesses. Administrators were encouraged to read management books and to attend seminars espousing ways to implement business practices and techniques in schools. The business model was touted as an approach superior to the system under which public schools had been operating. This movement received a substantial amount of media attention for several years.

Several other strategies have been proposed to "fix" public schools, and many of these would actually diminish the scope of public education or do away with it entirely. Among the suggestions were vouchers, which were initially targeted toward parochial and other private school parents. Vouchers would provide either a cash grant or tax credit to permit parents to either enroll their children in private schools or to subsidize those families with children already enrolled. This was one of the first choice options introduced into the national dialogue. Many public school educators believed vouchers to be a clear violation of the separation of church and state and could not believe such an approach would ever be declared legal, but there have been instances where some states have permitted a version of vouchers to be implemented. The most recent iteration of the approach is termed the Educational Savings Account (ESA).

Other options that were proposed to give parents more choice for their children have included homeschooling, magnet schools, open enrollment, and charter schools. Magnet schools were established in many school districts to either give parents a choice to send their children to a "theme" school or as a means of racially balancing some schools by enticing "majority" parents to send their children to schools in minority neighborhoods. Magnet schools typically operated within the confines of public school districts. Open enrollment, either within or across school district boundaries is another option promoting choice, and this concept also operates within the public school system. One of the elements of NCLB is the choice option, which is a modified version of open enrollment. The issue with this option is that another school district must agree to accept students from a failing district.

Charter schools are the option currently in vogue. While most charters operate under the auspices of public school districts, receiving their charters from those districts, they may actually be operated by private corporations. Charter schools in other locations are supervised by boards of directors consisting primarily of parents. The legislation allowing charter schools is more permissive in some states than others. Some charter schools are established with a specialized focus and others are more general.

While options such as vouchers, open enrollment, and charter schools may seem to be visible to the public, the forces behind these options constitute a shadow educational system. There are private individuals, corporations, and foundations spending millions of dollars in the attempt to influence public opinion regarding public education, often first through governmental leaders. Legally, there is probably little doubt that these individuals and foundations have the right to spend their money to influence public policy. Their right to do so was strengthened by the U.S.

Supreme Court's decision in the *Citizens United v. Federal Election Commission* case in 2010. While this case said that corporations are people in terms of certain campaign rights, it broadened the interpretation of corporations and foundations as people.

A major problem for public education is that many public school administrators and school boards are going through life oblivious to the existence of these individuals and groups. They do not know that much of the school reform movement, such as the current redesign of principal preparation programs, is being heavily influenced by private foundations. While some of the ideas being promoted by private individuals and groups may be good, their overall agenda may not be supportive of public education. Over the past thirty years, the professional educators have lost the initiative and their standing as experts regarding education. Now public education in many states is being run by governors and state legislatures rather than state superintendents and state boards of education. These state-level educational officials are primarily the proxies of governmental officials. In many cases, the governmental officials, and hence the state boards of education, are receiving their marching orders from the aforementioned private individuals and groups.

A VOUCHER BY ANY OTHER NAME

One of the first individuals to promote the use of vouchers in education was the famous economist, Milton Friedman. Friedman won the Nobel Prize in Economics in 1976. While vouchers were never really instituted in a major fashion during his lifetime, the Friedman Foundation for Educational Choice continues his legacy of promoting school vouchers. Under the new terminology of the Friedman Foundation for Educational Choice, vouchers are now called Educational Savings Accounts (ESAs). Before discussing the current status of ESAs, it will first be instructive to review the history and concepts of the voucher movement in the United States.

It has been a practice in several states, particularly in New England, for those school districts without high schools to give stipends to their high school–age resident students to attend either public high schools in neighboring districts, or private high schools. Generally, these private schools must be nonsectarian. It was not until the 1990s that a few cities and some states began experimenting with expanded voucher plans. The first publicly funded voucher plan was initiated in 1990 to provide state-funded vouchers for low-income students in Milwaukee. Initially, students were permitted to transfer to the nonsectarian private schools of their choice, but in 1995, this was expanded to include religious schools. Also in 1995, a voucher program was established for low-income students in Cleveland that authorized families to enroll their children in private schools.

The first attempt at a statewide voucher program was in Florida, beginning in 1999. Initially, the Florida plan gave vouchers, through its Opportunity Scholarship Program (OSP), to families of students attending failing schools, and two years later, this was expanded to enable students with disabilities to attend private schools. In the mid-2000s, Ohio expanded the Cleveland program into a statewide program and Utah initiated a statewide program for students with disabilities. Several states also offer tax credits or tax deductions to compensate residents who have either acquired expenses in private and, sometimes, public schools or those who have donated to a private tuition scholarship fund. The establishment or the attempt to establish voucher programs has led to a number of state and federal court cases. Two U.S. Supreme Court cases are worth mentioning, because they have influenced subsequent state court cases.

Opponents of voucher plans typically claim that state support of private schools is a violation of the establishment clause of the First Amendment to the U.S. Constitution. Until the beginning of the voucher movement, it had generally been the conventional wisdom among public school educators and advocates that the use of public funds to support private education was not permissible. However, in *Zelman v. Simmons-Harris* (2002), the U.S. Supreme Court upheld the Cleveland scholarship voucher program on a 5–4 vote. The majority ruled that this plan was a religiously neutral approach to giving school choice options to parents residing within the boundaries of the Cleveland City School District. In the majority's opinion, this satisfied the establishment clause constitutional issue. However, this was a permissive ruling and did not state that all voucher plans would meet the constitutional test. Indeed, in the dissenting opinion, Justice Souter stated that the majority had gone too far and alerted state and federal legislators to the threats generated by the practice of issuing publicly supported vouchers for use in private schools.

The *Zelman* ruling was soon followed by another Supreme Court case, *Locke v. Davey* (2004). In a 7–2 decision, the Court upheld the right of states to be even stricter than required by the establishment clause in prohibiting financial assistance to religious institutions. This reinforced the right of states to make laws that are unique to their own conditions and circumstances. Rather than having one approach to vouchers, we may well have many differing approaches. It is interesting that in some of the cases in which it was found that vouchers do not violate the establishment clause of the First Amendment, the rationale was that the money was going to parents who then exercised their choice to enroll their children in private and religious schools. Essentially, no state funds were going "directly" to religious institutions.

Most of Florida's OSP program was invalidated by the Florida Supreme Court in 2006. The upper court avoided the establishment clause issue in its decision. Rather, the majority in *Bush v. Holmes* stated that the Florida constitution called for a system of high quality and a uniform system of public education across the state. Since the private schools were not required to administer statewide assessments and since private school teachers were not required to obtain state certification, the 5–2 majority ruled that voucher programs do not adequately provide for a uniform education across the state. The court did not invalidate the use of state funds by disabled students in private schools.

A pilot Colorado voucher program was invalidated in 2004 because the Colorado Supreme Court found the program violated Colorado's local control provision of the state constitution. The court also stated that it took away the ability of local boards of education to control their own finances. Even though Colorado is generally permissive regarding parental choice, the high court did not uphold vouchers in that state. These are just a few examples of court decisions pertaining to the use of vouchers. Clearly, this remains a fluid situation and varies from state to state.

In a 2012 report prepared for the Friedman Foundation for Educational Choice, Matthew Ladner decries the failure of the American public schools and blames this decline on the monopoly of the public schools and on unionization. He calls the achievement gap between white and minority students a national disgrace and blames this on the public schools, avoiding a discussion of socioeconomics. Ladner proposes ESAs as an answer. In a review of this report, Charisse Gulosino and Jonah Liebert (2012) counter many of the claims posited in Ladner's report, stating that "None of the 25 citations are to an independent, peer-reviewed study" (2012, p. 3). They go on to state that many of the citations are from partisan sources.

Arizona has experimented with the concept of ESAs. Originally targeting Arizona's students with disabilities, the expanded version of the Arizona Empowerment Scholarship Accounts, are now also available to students in schools graded D or F under Arizona's accountability system, as well as students having gone through the foster care system and children of active-duty military personnel. Conceivably, this program could now encompass up to 20 percent of Arizona's school-age population. This program is facing court challenges. The ultimate fate of this voucher system under a new name will most likely rest with the Arizona court system.

Advocates of vouchers claim the provision of vouchers gives low-income families more choice in the education of their children. Advocates also claim instilling this type of competition into the system will improve the quality of all schools, including public schools. Essentially, advocates propose that this will lead to the survival of the fittest. At this point, there is a dearth of research-based evidence regarding the efficacy of vouchers in improving the educational performance of students. There is also little doubt that when parents have a choice in choosing schools for their children, they are more likely to be supportive of the selected schools and of the educational process.

Opponents of vouchers fear a widespread implementation of voucher systems across the country will dilute the democratizing effect of public schools. They reason this type of shift, enabling more parents to choose their schools, will lead to more homogeneous schools, since parents will seek schools that enforce their beliefs and values. The trend toward resegregation has already been addressed in this book. While the desire to find like-minded individuals in a school setting is not necessarily bad, there is also little doubt that those parents already interested in and supportive of education will be the most active in seeking out alternatives for their children, regardless of income. Critics of vouchers assert that the fiscal incentives are often not enough to enable or entice low-income families to move their children into a new school setting.

HOMESCHOOLING

Homeschooling has increased from just a blip on the radar screen in the 1980s to a major phenomenon in today's educational environment. By one estimate, 2,040,000 students were being homeschooled in the United States in 2010 (Ray, 2011, p. 3). This would constitute approximately 3.8 percent of the U.S. school-age population. However, the number of children being homeschooled is very difficult to track. Only thirteen states consistently collect data on homeschooled children. Even with that, it is estimated that as many as 10 percent of homeschooling families are underground and fail to inform the state they are homeschooling; even in those states where registration is required (Ray, 2011, p. 3).

Since there is still a dearth of systematic data pertaining to the demographic composition of homeschooling population, it is impossible to pinpoint the exact composition of this group. However, some (Ray, 1990, Rudner, 1999) have stated the homeschooling population is typically Caucasian and middle class. In a 2007 study of 136 homeschooling parents, Green and Hoover-Dempsey found that only 5 percent of their subjects were non-Caucasian, 58 percent held a four-year college degree and their family income averaged over $50,000 per year (p. 267). The comparison group of public school parents in the same study was much more diverse and less college-educated, and they had a much lower income level. Clearly, more research is needed regarding the demographics of homeschool participation.

Families choose to homeschool their children for a variety of reasons. Some make this choice primarily for religious reasons, and in a sometimes related rationale, some parents wish to protect their children from the influences found in the world of public schooling. There are parents who believe they can give their children individual attention and consequently believe that homeschooling is the right decision for their families. Such parents may actually be supportive of the public schools. Other parents, while supporters of public schooling in general, are not happy with the schools in their own neighborhoods. Yet other parents homeschool their children because that is what most people in their particular church or social circle have chosen.

Green and Hoover-Dempsey (2007) found that parents of homeschooled students appear to be motivated by wanting to be actively involved in the lives of their children and had a strong sense of efficacy for helping their children learn (p. 264). This study also found parents' decisions to homeschool their children were not overwhelmingly influenced by their beliefs regarding the content, instructional methods, effectiveness, and values of public education. They were more motivated by their personal sense of efficacy. Other studies (Bielick, et al., 2001; Collom, 2005) suggest that there may be a shift occurring from primarily ideological reasons for homeschooling to more pedagogical reasons. The growth of curriculum designed for homeschooling families has made homeschooling a more practical option for many families.

Some school administrators have had concerns with homeschooling because it is so unregulated. In certain cases, administrators have suspected parents have not adequately educated their children at home. Many educators express concern that homeschooled children miss out on socialization activities and that they will have a hard time adjusting to real-life situations when they are adults. Another issue is the quality of curriculum that homeschooled children are subjected to as well as a lack of standardized testing of homeschooled children in some states, taking away one measure of accountability for student progress. What happens when and if homeschooled children enter or come back into the public school environment? In other cases, there may be some school district administrators upset over the state aid that is lost for each student not enrolled in the public schools, although districts still receive the local property tax revenues from homeschooling families.

The regulation of homeschooling varies widely among the states. Some states essentially have no regulations and are perceived to be the most homeschool-friendly locations for this activity. These states require no notification, although some may ask that parents volunteer the information that they are homeschooling. They really have no oversight of homeschooling curriculum and do not require state assessments of homeschooled students. Among these least regulated states are Alaska, Connecticut, Idaho, Illinois, Indiana, Michigan, Missouri, New Jersey, Oklahoma, and Texas.

At the next level are states that have a low level of homeschool regulation. The primary requirement in such states is notification of the state that parents will be homeschooling their children. There are no other requirements such as testing, home visits, or other reporting. States falling into this category are Alabama, Arizona, California, Delaware, Kansas, Kentucky, Mississippi, Montana, Nebraska, Nevada, New Mexico, Utah, Wisconsin, and Wyoming. Washington, D.C., also falls within this group.

A third category of states have what might be termed moderate regulations, and are not felt to be homeschool friendly. These states require written notification of homeschool activities to the local school district. They also require state standardized test scores from homeschooled students. Professional evaluation of homeschoolers' performance is required, and if the home school district believes the homeschool is not meeting its obligations, then it could revoke that family's right to homeschool. States falling within this category are Arkansas, Colorado, Florida, Georgia, Hawaii, Iowa, Louisiana, Maine, Maryland, Minnesota, New Hampshire, North Carolina, Ohio, Oregon, South Carolina, South Dakota, Tennessee, Virginia, Washington, and West Virginia.

The final group of states is those with strict requirements for homeschooling families. In addition to notification, mandatory state testing, and professional evaluation, these states may also require approval of curriculum, reporting of attendance hours, and general student progress, and may even require the parents to hold teacher certification. Some states even require home visits by school officials. Obviously, such states are not considered to be homeschool friendly by most homeschooling parents. States falling into this category are Massachusetts, New York, North Dakota, Pennsylvania, Rhode Island, and Vermont.

Homeschooling parents occasionally ask the local school district for permission for their children to enroll in specific classes or to participate in a variety of activities. The ability to enroll in advanced mathematics or science courses is not an unusual request. Other typical requests involve participation in music and physical education courses. When parents request the opportunity for their children to become involved in student activities, the situation may become much trickier. Often, sports and other activities are regulated by state activities associations; typically at the high school level, but also at the middle school level in some states.

Thus, interscholastic activities decisions may actually be beyond the control of the school principal, superintendent, or even the local board of education. While the attitude toward homeschooling varies from state to state and community to community, an increasing number of school officials are working with, rather than against, homeschooling parents. In a sense, the relationship between public school officials and homeschooling families is analogous to the relationship such administrators and board members have with private and parochial school parents. Often these parents are taxpayers. Ultimately, the public school flexibility benefits the child.

A previously mentioned criticism of the homeschool movement is the lack of socialization activities for students schooled at home. In increasing numbers of locations, parents work hard to provide socialization activities. For example, in Springfield, Missouri, the homeschool orchestra has approximately 350 participants (Elizabeth Suh, personal communication, February 28, 2013). Other activities for homeschoolers in the Springfield area include sports teams, a graduation ceremony, prom, and cooperative classes organized by parents. Classes such as English, science, art, and physical education are cooperatively taught by parents and give students interaction opportunities.

Some high school–age students also take community college classes as a means of addressing more advanced courses. Another interesting phenomenon of the homeschool movement is the trading of goods and services. Trading babysitting for music lessons or tutoring would be one good example. Other parents trade home-produced food products for services. Homeschooling parents are increasingly finding ways to promote socialization activities, and a homeschooled student taught in complete isolation is probably rare today.

Research has been conducted regarding how well homeschooled students score on nationally standardized tests in those situations where they take these tests. In particular, studies have been conducted (Frost, 1987; Rakestraw, 1987; Wartes, 1990; Ray, 1990; Rudner, 1999) on how well students perform on the Iowa Tests of Basic Skills and the Stanford Achievement Test. Homeschooled students outperformed their public school contemporaries at nearly all grade levels according to these studies. Another researcher (Galloway, 1995) found that homeschooled students outperformed their private school peers on the English subtest of the ACT. While this research is limited, it is some indication that students are learning and growing academically in the homeschooling environment.

The question is often raised regarding how well homeschooled students will perform at the college level. This is a question raised by parents as well as educators. Two researchers (Jones & Gloeckner, 2004) compared fifty-five first-year homeschooled graduates with fifty-three traditional (public, private, and parochial) high school graduates on grade point average, retention, ACT Test scores, and credits earned after their first year of college in Colorado four-year public universities or colleges. Although not statistically significant, the average grade point averages, credits earned, and ACT composite scores were all higher than those of their traditional school peers after the first year (p. 20). While this research was limited in scope, it did seem to show that homeschooled students could perform well at the college level.

Clearly, homeschooling is not for everyone. It may be financially impossible for some families; particularly single-parent households. It takes a real commitment by participating parents to be organized, seek out and implement a solid curriculum, and organize social activities for their children. Perhaps as much as anything, it takes organizational skills to make this approach to education work. However, it seems to be working for a growing number of American families. In recent years, homeschooled students have won the National Geography Bee and the National Spelling Bee, as well as other contests. The issue of high school credits and college admission has also become a nonissue with many institutions of higher education.

CHARTER SCHOOLS

Charter schools have received mixed reviews since their inception. The basic premise of a charter school is that it has the ability to operate with fewer restrictions than its traditional public school peers. Most often, charter schools are granted their charters by the public school district within whose boundaries the charter school is to be located. In other instances, the charter may be held by other entities, such as universities. The charter schools may actually be directed by a board of directors or governors, comprised of parents and other interested constituents, or the school may be operated by a private corporation.

States have varying regulations pertaining to the establishment of charter schools, and some states are more permissive than others in this regard. Most states have a limit, or cap, on the number of charter schools that may be established. Some states encourage or require that charter schools be established in low-income and urban areas, and in some cases charters may be established with specific purposes in mind. For example, some urban charters target students that have had limited success in traditional public schools. Two Midwestern states with fairly restrictive charter guidelines are Missouri and Illinois.

All of Missouri's charter schools are confined to Kansas City and St. Louis. In 2013, Kansas City had 9,577 students enrolled in twenty-two separate charter schools. St. Louis had 8,482 students enrolled in sixteen charter schools. However, the Confluence Academy had multiple sites and enrolled 3,084 of the 8,482 total. Thus, the two largest cities in Missouri had just over 18,000 students enrolled in charter schools. This is a very small proportion of the public school population in Missouri.

Missouri's neighboring state to the east, Illinois, is only slightly more permissive regarding charter schools. A bulk of Illinois's fifty-two charter schools are located in Chicago. Thirty-eight of the charter providers are located within the boundaries of Chicago Public School District 299. Thirteen of Illinois's 867 school districts have charter schools, and in addition to Chicago, most of these are in urban settings such as Peoria, Springfield, and East St. Louis. A handful are in smaller communities. Just over forty-nine thousand Illinois K–12 students were in charter schools in 2011, which is about 2.4 percent of the total public school population of just over two million students.

Eleven percent of the students within the Chicago Public Schools boundaries are enrolled in charter schools. As previously mentioned, some charter schools are special-focus schools. The UNO charter schools in Chicago, for example, are dedicated to integrating Latina/o students into American life. The UNO network hosts eleven Chicago charter schools, making it the second largest provider in the state, with approximately fifty-five hundred students. There are critics who complain that in some states, charter schools are only located in low-income urban areas, with the implication that while charters may be good enough for poor urban youth, they are not appropriate for suburban students.

Contrast Illinois and Missouri with the charter school situation in Colorado. In 2013, over eighty thousand Colorado K–12 students were attending more than one hundred ninety charter school campuses throughout the state, constituting nearly 11 percent of the total K–12 enrollment in Colorado (Colorado League of Charter Schools, 2013). Colorado charter schools are distributed throughout the state in all types of districts. Many districts have chartered multiple charter schools and more are being added each year. In Colorado, charter school teachers must be "highly qualified" under the NCLB regulations. Colorado charter schools enroll a wide range of students, with 45.4 percent coming from minority families. This is 2.5 percent higher than the percent of minority students enrolled in the state's traditional schools.

Why is Colorado so receptive to the charter school movement? Perhaps this attitude is related to the fact that Colorado has been an open-enrollment state since 1991. This essentially means that any student may attend any public school in the state as long as there is room and as long as parents or guardians can provide transportation to the new site. Colorado has not had a strong union tradition as a state. The legislature and the courts in Colorado have long been supportive of the charter school movement. Colorado also has a strong charter advocacy group known as the Colorado League of Charter Schools, which provides technical and legal assistance to individuals and groups interested in initiating charter schools.

Just how effective are charter schools? In recent years, there have been varying accounts of the success or failure of charter schools and one of the most commonly recurring themes is that charter schools are no more effective and are often less effective than the public schools in the same communities in which charter schools are located. In 2009, the Center for Research on Education Outcomes (CREDO) at Stanford University released a major study entitled, "Multiple Choice: Charter School Performance in 16 States." This was one of the first comprehensive studies that addressed the issue of charter school effectiveness. This study was unique because it was able through statistical techniques to compare the learning of charter school students in sixteen states with the learning experiences they would have had in the traditional schools they would have otherwise attended (CREDO, 2009, p. 1). An interesting aspect of this study was the researchers were able to develop virtual twins for 84 percent of all students in charter schools, for comparison purposes.

The CREDO researchers estimated they were able to analyze the impact of charter school attendance on more than 70 percent of charter school attendees nationwide. The findings on charter school performance were mixed, but with a number of significant points. The researchers compared reading and mathematics results of the charter school students and their virtual peers. The results showed that 17 percent of charter schools provided superior educational opportunities to students. Almost half of the charter schools provided similar opportunities to their students, but 37 percent of charter schools provided educational opportunities that were significantly worse than their public school peers (CREDO, 2009, p. 1).

The CREDO results were not universal, and varied by state and among various subgroups of students. At the state level, the researchers found that the existence of caps on the number of charter schools depresses student achievement results. Similarly, states with large numbers of providers seem to have lower achievement, but those states with an appeals process regarding the establishment of charters have higher student achievement (CREDO, 2009, pp. 40–41). Overall, this research seemed to present a mixed set of evidence pertaining to charter schools. When examined by state, the picture becomes somewhat clearer.

How did this translate into charter school achievement, state-by-state? In five states, charter school students experienced significantly higher growth than their traditional public school peers. These states were Arkansas, Colorado, Illinois, Louisiana, and Missouri. In Arizona, Florida, Minnesota, New Mexico, Ohio, and Texas, the learning gains of charter school students were lower than the gains of their public school peers. There was no significant difference in the learning results of charter and noncharter students in California, the District of Columbia, Georgia, and North Carolina (CREDO, 2009, p. 45).

The findings also showed significant learning differences among charter school attendees from various subgroups. Overall, students from low-income homes and those that were English Language Learners (ELL) performed better than their public school peers. Minority students in charter schools, specifically African Americans and Latina/os did not perform as well as their traditional public school peers (CREDO, 2009, p. 45). Considering the fact that to be a minority also means that you are more likely to have a low income in this country, this possible contradiction is difficult to explain. Continuing research is needed in this area, particularly if the expansion of charter schools is a consideration.

It is safe to say that some charter schools are more successful than others, but poorly performing charter schools may be doing their students a disservice. It is possible that those students would be receiving a better education in their traditional public schools. On the other hand, if the traditional public schools in some of these neighborhoods are also failing their students, then the difference among schools may be relative. It has proven difficult in some locations to close those charter schools not performing up to expectations because once parents send their children to a charter school, that school becomes their school. It has been their choice to utilize that school, and academics may not be the only reason parents select a school. It has been easier to close charter schools because they are having financial difficulties than for the poor performance of their students.

Other charter schools outperform their traditional public school counterparts. This may be due to their focus or theme or because of the leadership of the school, including involved parents. Some charter schools are located in states that are more amenable to the charter school process. Some charter schools are doing a better job of educating their low-income and ELL students. Other charter schools and traditional public schools need to analyze what the successful charters schools are doing with these students and replicate those approaches to the extent possible.

PRIVATE INDIVIDUALS AND GROUPS

Much of the public and many educational administrators do not understand the extent to which the American public school system is under attack today. More explicitly, they are unaware of the sources of many of these attacks. Administrators understand that the public perception of the public schools has become tarnished over the past few decades, but many still struggle to ascertain exactly why the attacks have become so strident and so frequent. Since there is such a consistent denigration of the public schools, there is a natural tendency on the part of many people to believe that a vast majority of the public schools must be failing. While this may not seem to be true to many individual parents who are pleased with the schools their own children attend, many think that most other public schools must be in real trouble.

School administrators have a broader perspective regarding the quality of the public schools than much of the public, and the experience of many administrators tells them that the schools are stronger than the public image. Administrators talk among themselves, they visit other schools, and these conversations and visits often belie the image of failing schools. At the same time, administrators know the negative public perception is out there, but they are not quite certain why. School administrators work in jobs filled with stress and conflict. Even though they believe schools are stronger than they are portrayed to be by the public and the media, becoming involved in one more stressful confrontation over the quality of schools is one conflict that administrators can, and often do, avoid. While they may occasionally defend their own schools or school districts, they often avoid broader discussions on this topic.

Educators as well as the general public need to understand this attack on education is not random; it is well financed and coordinated. Much of the current criticism of the American public schools comes from a neoliberal agenda that is quite strong in contemporary U.S. society. Neoliberalism is a political philosophy favoring open markets, economic liberalization, privatization, and free trade. Neoliberals prefer the expansion of the private sector with a concurrent decrease in the size of the public sector. This applies as much to schooling as to other areas of life. Many private individuals and groups have spent years financially supporting and building up organizations that are in the business of supporting this agenda.

According to Fenwick English, five of the most prominent individuals promoting neoliberal thinking vis-à-vis public education are Chester Finn, Frederick Hess, Eli Broad, Louis Gerstner, and Arne Duncan (English, 2010, p. 3). These individuals either work for conservative foundations, support foundations, or write about education. Of course, Arne Duncan is the current U.S. secretary of education. Both as the CEO of the Chicago Public Schools and as the secretary of education, Mr. Duncan has supported various neoliberal approaches such as charter schools, alternative licensing, merit pay for increased student achievement on tests, and decreasing the influence of teacher unions. His agenda has continued with the implementation of RTTT.

There are a number of neoliberal or conservative foundations that work to influence education in the United States. For example, the Thomas B. Fordham Foundation, whose president is Chester Finn, is financially supported by the Broad Foundation. Finn has also had a relationship with the Edison Project, which manages charter schools and school districts in nearly twenty states. Eli and Edythe Broad are both heavily involved in the reform of public education and have funded initiatives such as the Broad Superintendents Academy and the Broad Residency in Urban Education, which both train nontraditional candidates for superintendencies or other central office leadership positions. Frederick Hess is the director of Education Policy Studies at the American Enterprise Institute. Louis Gerstner, former CEO of IBM, has advocated for the elimination of public school districts and school boards.

Other privately funded foundations, centers, and institutes have been used by their proponents to promote a private agenda and to attack the public schools. Among these additional organizations are the Business Roundtable, the Center for the Study of American Business, the Cato Institute, the Devos Foundation, the Heritage Foundation, the Hoover

Institution, the John Olin Foundation, the Lynde and Harry Bradley Foundation, the Manhattan Institute, the Sarah Schaife Foundation, and the Smith Richardson Foundation. The Wal-Mart Foundation has been one of the largest advocates of the promotion of school vouchers (Kumashiro, 2008, p. 13). These groups work within their own membership and beyond, through their funding initiatives and publicity to shape public education policy. Much of this is done with the expressed purpose of preparing a competitive workforce for the future.

Two groups deserving particular attention are the Wallace Foundation and the Southern Regional Education Board. The Wallace Foundation was founded with funds provided by DeWitt and Lila Acheson Wallace, the heirs to the *Readers Digest* fortune. The initial purpose of the Wallace Foundation was to improve education and the lives of disadvantaged children. Around 2000, the Wallace Foundation decided to shift its focus from simply "doing good" to attempting to make and influence change when a major focus became developing and sharing ideas on school leadership. One of Wallace's first major efforts in this area was the State Action for Education Leadership Project (SAELP). When rolling out SAELP, Wallace worked in concert with the Council of Chief State School Officers (CCSSO), the National Governors Association, the National Conference of State Legislatures, the National Association of State Boards of Education, and the Education Commission of the States.

In 2001, Wallace funded the first SAELP cohort of fifteen states with a grant of $8.9 million. In 2004, this was followed by another grant of $3.6 million. The Wallace funding was successful in influencing state policy pertaining to administrative leadership in some cases. The fact that Wallace established relationships, at the very beginning, with state superintendents and boards of education made it much more likely that Wallace would exert a major degree of influence on state policies, and states went about the business of the reform of school administration preparation programs. While there is no doubt that some of the Wallace initiatives proved to be positive in terms of education and school administration specifically, Wallace's influence was largely unknown outside of legislative and state board circles.

Illinois is a prime example of a state where Wallace funding made a major impact. The Illinois SAELP group, or I-SAELP, received an initial $50,000 planning grant and a subsequent $250,000 grant from the Wallace Foundation. The I-SAELP was housed in the Center for the Study of Education Policy at Illinois State University. Through the years, I-SAELP lobbied the legislature and the Illinois State Board of Education for changes in principal preparation programs. After an initial School Leader Task Force was formed, a subsequent ad hoc committee worked from 2008 through 2010 on suggestions for the redesign of principal preparation programs in Illinois.

Members of the I-SAELP were involved in every meeting of this committee, and were present when testimony was given by participants at the Illinois State Board of Education meeting when the recommendations from the committee were presented. There is no doubt that when several committee recommendations were modified or eliminated, the I-SAELP staff played an influential role. Over the years, I-SAELP staff had gained access to staff members of the Illinois State Board of Education, as well as to members of the board of education. This influx of funding to I-SAELP came at the very time when Illinois was in the throes of a terrible fiscal crisis. While most educational administrators were in their home trying to keep their buildings and districts afloat, the I-SAELP staff members were assuming the role of "educational experts" in the state.

The Wallace Foundation has also given financial support to the Southern Regional Education Board (SREB). SREB was established in 1948 by Southern governors and legislators to promote education in their region. Sixteen states currently belong to SREB, and the committee membership is comprised of the governors of those sixteen states along with four additional appointees from each state. Of those four, one must be a legislator and another must be an educator. The 2012–2013 board chair was Governor Bobby Jindal of Louisiana. The SREB staff members produce many reports and materials meant to influence the manner in which school administrators are prepared and how they conduct their work.

A recent review of the SREB website showed fifty-one publications related to school leadership. Among the illustrative titles included in that section are the following three books:

- *Preparing a New Breed of Principals: It's Time for Action*
- *The Principal Internship: How Can We Get It Right?*
- *Good Principals Aren't Born—They're Mentored: Are We Investing Enough to Get the School Leaders We Need?*

It is obvious from these titles, and others published by SREB, that the organization is all about promoting change. It is important to note that SREB is taking its message beyond the borders of the sixteen states included in its membership. In addition to exporting its materials to other states, it sends representative staff members to spread the word about its ideas for leadership change.

This happened in Illinois. When the aforementioned ad hoc task force was working on proposed changes in Illinois principal preparation programs, SREB representatives presented a "packaged" approach at one of the initial meetings. The task force discounted the sales pitch and decided to develop its own model, but after the task force had completed its work, materials from SREB were inserted into Section 23 of the Illinois Administrative Code. It was specifically stated that training programs for principals serving as mentors for interns as well as faculty supervisors should "align with the 13 critical success factors and the 36 associated competencies outlined in 'The Principal Internship: How Can We Get It Right?'" (Illinois State Board of Education, 2013), which is published by SREB. Some of the critical success factors and associated competencies mentioned above may have value, but the manner in which they were imposed, through externally funded lobbying efforts, certainly has deflated the sense of empowerment initially felt by those public and private school professors, administrators, and teachers involved in the principal redesign process.

One of the most recent neoliberal initiatives being promoted within several states is the move to tie some portion of teacher and principal evaluation to student academic achievement. A stimulus for this movement was the carrot provided by the possibility of receiving RTTT funding. Numerous states rushed to submit proposals for funding that included some sort of student achievement-evaluation link. This was accompanied in some cases by legislative action. In Illinois, such legislation was submitted, approved, and signed by the governor within approximately a twenty-four-hour time period. Even though the state has not received RTTT funding, a portion of principal and teacher evaluation is now linked to student achievement.

A VOICE OF EXPERIENCE

The author's first contact with homeschooling came when he was a central office administrator in a school district in Colorado Springs when one of his roles was to track the level of homeschooling being exercised by the parents within the school district. District officials began to see a significant growth in homeschooling numbers beginning around 1990, and over a period of three years, the district experienced an increase from approximately twenty families to over two hundred families. Perhaps Colorado Springs was one of the areas in the forefront of this movement because it was a very conservative community. In addition to a very large military presence, Colorado Springs began seeing an influx of conservative religious organizations establishing their headquarters in the Colorado Springs area. Colorado is one of the states requiring registration and achievement testing of homeschooled students, thus the district had a fairly good count of the number of families involved.

Over the years, an increasing number of administrators have come to accept homeschooling as a legitimate alternative method of education that works for many families. An early concern with homeschooling was homeschooled students would miss out on socialization activities, but homeschool organizations in many communities have attempted to overcome this by providing joint activities for homeschooled children such as group activities, field trips, and so on. A large percent of school districts now allow resident homeschooled students to participate in a variety of student activities, and certain classes such as art, music, physical education, and particular specialized classes that parents may feel are beyond their capabilities to adequately teach. Most districts accept such students because they recognize the parents may be district taxpayers and they know such flexibility will benefit students. In virtually all cases, homeschooled students must accommodate their schedules to meet the school's schedule. One remaining area of difficulty can be the participation of homeschooled students in interscholastic athletics, which are generally supervised by state activities associations.

In the spirit of full disclosure, the author believes there is a place for choice within the U.S. system of public education. He may be one of the few people in the country that served as the director of two separate K–12 university laboratory schools, one in Missouri and the other in Colorado. One of his children attended the laboratory school in Colorado. When the family returned to Illinois, all three of the author's children attended a magnet school within the public school system where he worked. In the case of that district, the magnet school provided a bit of friendly competition to the other schools within the district.

In this chapter, the author spent some time addressing the concept of charter schools. It can be a viable concept when initiated by parents rather than some large corporation. The author knows from personal experience that charter schools generally work well in Colorado, especially those that are chartered by the local public school district. Since Colorado has been an open-enrollment state since the very early 1990s, charter schools seemed like the next logical choice for parents in that state. Many Colorado public school districts have accepted charter schools as an accepted part of the educational landscape.

Finally, as stated earlier in this chapter, the author believes the U.S. system of public education is under direct attack from a number of neoliberal and conservative individuals and groups. School administrators can no longer go through life ignoring the influence of these individuals and groups. Public school building and district administrators have lost the voice of authority and the moral high ground as spokespersons of public education. It is time for educational administrators to address this issue. Suggestions for remedying this situation are proposed in the final chapter.

SUMMARY

This chapter addressed the shadow system in education, including vouchers, homeschooling, charter schools, and the influence of private individuals and groups on public education policy. As with most things, the concepts addressed in this chapter have both positive and negative elements. The term *shadow system* was not meant to be used in a derogatory fashion. Rather, it was used to imply that many people, including educators, are not fully aware of many of the activities described. At the very least, the public needs to be made aware of the basis of support of these alternatives.

While vouchers may have fallen out of vogue, there are periodic attempts to revive this approach to funding parental choice. The most recent iteration is called the Education Savings Account (ESA). Public school advocates have balked at the voucher approach, especially when public dollars were to be used to fund parochial schools. In *Zelman v. Simmons-Harris* (2002) the U.S. Supreme Court upheld the use of vouchers in parochial schools based upon the premise that the money was being channeled through parents, and parental choice, to the parochial schools. However, in 2007, the U.S. Supreme Court ruled in *Locke v. Davey* that individual states could be even stricter than required by the establishment clause in establishing guidelines prohibiting the use of public funds to assist parochial schools.

Homeschooling is as old as the American republic. However, with the growth of public, private and parochial schools, most Americans sent their children to schools outside the home. After the Civil War, and increasing in intensity during the Industrial Revolution, the concept of institutionalized schooling grew. Beginning in the 1980s, increasing numbers of Americans began to choose to educate their children at home. Parents make this choice for numerous and differing reasons.

At the present time, it is estimated that over two million school-aged children are educated at home. States vary in the degree of control that they exercise over homeschooling, with some not even requiring registration and with those states at the other extreme implementing very strict monitoring and supervision activities. While some parents homeschool their children because they disagree with the values and practices of the public schools, it appears a growing number of parents engage in this practice because they have the time, resources, and inclination to homeschool their children and may actually be supportive of the public schools. Many companies now provide curricular materials directed to homeschooling parents. Homeschooling parents in many communities have found ways to provide socialization activities for their youngsters.

The legislation pertaining to charter schools varies widely by state. In some states, charter schools are essentially limited to urban areas and primarily enroll minority and low-income students. Many times, such schools are targeted or limited in their mission. In other states, the number of charter schools is not severely capped by number or location and may enroll a wider demographic in terms of students accepted. Colorado was cited as one state that is very permissive, with over one hundred ninety charter schools, and educating approximately 11 percent of the Colorado school-aged population.

Some charter schools are operated by for-profit businesses and others are essentially run by parental boards of governors. Student achievement in charter schools is mixed, with some doing better than the public schools in their neighborhoods, some performing about the same, and others falling below the public school performance. In one major study, low-income students enrolled in charter schools performed better academically than their public school peers. Overall, the results are mixed in this area. More research is needed if charters are to be expanded.

Finally, the influence of private individuals and private groups on public education policy was examined. The current neoliberal and conservative successful attempts to influence educational policy were examined. Current influential individuals were mentioned and more attention was directed toward the influence of private groups such as the Wallace Foundation and the Southern Regional Education Board (SREB). While some of the ideas of these individuals and groups may be positive, many Americans do not understand the scope of the funding these individuals and groups are providing to influence public educational policy. While the influence of these groups may be either positive or negative, the extent of their activities needs to become public knowledge.

FOUR
Administrative Decision Making: Conflict or Consensus?

Administrators at all levels in any school building or district are faced with a myriad of situations requiring decisions on a daily basis. Of course, not all of these are major decisions, but even the cumulative effect of these minor decisions can be tiring. Conversely, some of the major decisions administrators must make can be career altering; not always in a positive direction. While many postings for administrative openings list consensus building near the top of the list of preferred attributes, is building consensus always the best decision-making model in the organization? Are there still times when decisions should be made in a "top-down" fashion?

Decision making through consensus building or collaboration, while often effective, can be a very time-consuming process. The same board of education that listed consensus building as a strongly desired attribute in its new superintendent may want a major decision made tomorrow. In such a situation, we already have a conflict that requires resolution. Another consideration is that different situations may require alternate decision-making approaches. Making a decision about what to do when the building is on fire probably requires a different approach than deciding which reading series to implement in the school district. The author once worked with a boss in Colorado who talked about Level 1, Level 2, and Level 3 decisions; each of which called for differing decision-making strategies, depending upon the importance of the decision to the organization.

In the same Colorado school district, administrators were taught to look directionally when making decisions. Regardless of where you were situated in the organization, you first looked up for rationale when making a decision. Second, you looked horizontally for impact. If you implement a particular new approach or program in your school, as the building principal, what type of impact might this change have on the other schools in your district? Finally, we were taught to look down for support. You must have your troops with you as you implement change, either in your school or your district. How many times have administrators led a charge only to turn around and see that their troops were not following?

There is a school of thought that says conflict in organizations is not always a negative thing, as long as that conflict can be channeled to stimulate creative thinking and to generate new ideas. In other words, if an administrator can periodically create a bit of cognitive dissonance within the organization, helpful ideas and suggestions may emerge. Administrators must be skillful enough to manage conflict so it remains positive, or constructive, rather than negative, or destructive (Priem, Harrison, & Muir, 1995). In constructive conflict, administrators are able to facilitate the decision-making process in a fashion that allows the challenging of assumptions, beliefs, and ideas in a controlled situation where participants present and receive new ideas in an atmosphere of respect and individuals' feelings are left intact. Conversely, destructive conflict emerges when the group facilitator allows the conversation to get out of control and group members become emotional and angry during the discussion. Preventing this from happening often depends upon the establishment of firm ground rules before the conversation even begins and it requires strong group facilitation skills by the administrator.

Decision making through consensus is not always easy. Consensus building takes time if it is done correctly. The thinking behind the consensus approach is the more people involved in the process, the greater the amount of information being shared, thus expanding the group members' ability to understand the interests, expertise, and knowledge of other group members. This mutual understanding and trust theoretically leads to a variety of options that can be considered by the group in a nonthreatening atmosphere. Ultimately, final decisions derived through this process supposedly have a better chance of being supported by all involved in the process. This type of decision making is a foundation of the "win-win" negotiations process used by some school districts.

Another possible flaw in the consensus process is that you may not actually have true consensus. Some group members may be afraid to speak up in opposition to decisions derived in this fashion. Others may believe everyone else in the group supports the decision, so they decide not to complain in order to maintain harmony in the group. If there are enough of these individuals in the group, this may lead to problems for the leader and the decision later. Some facilitators lack the skills to discern this type of situation.

Managing administrative decision making through either consensus or conflict requires a strong set of skills, which will vary depending on the situation. A variety of studies (Hunt, Watkins, Kersten, & Tripses, 2011; Hunt, Kim, Watkins, & Tripses, 2013; Litchka & Polka, 2013) have shown that these skills are not currently adequately addressed in superintendent preparation programs. It seems developing these skills is more of an on-the-job training process, and some administrators learn more than others. This is a situation that needs to be addressed by those in charge of administrative preparation programs at all levels. If these skills are not being taught at the superintendent level, then it is highly unlikely things are being handled differently in principal preparation programs. In both cases, major improvements need to be implemented if we expect our future administrators to be effective decision makers, and in the same vein, there is little doubt that actively practicing school and district administrators need staff development in the area of conflict resolution and decision making.

WHO OWNS THE MONKEY?

When the author was an administrative team member in a fairly large school district, he had a boss who kept a toy monkey in his office. During administrative team meetings, while the team was discussing issues requiring decisions, the boss would periodically toss the monkey to an individual within the group, saying, "The monkey is now on your back." His point was that decisions need to be made at the appropriate level in the organization. There are times when teachers take on responsibilities that rightfully belong to their students. In the same fashion, principals often cover issues that really belong to teachers. Many administrators often become entrapped in a barrel of monkeys, taking responsibility for issues that should be handled by other team members.

There are administrators unwilling to distribute decision making because they believe they are ultimately accountable for the final decision. As President Harry Truman said, "The buck stops here." The problem with this approach is it diminishes what an administrator can handle. Anyone who has been a building-level or district administrator knows there are not enough hours in the day to handle all of the tasks on the plate. A sign of true leadership is the ability to assess the strengths of those in your organization and to assign significant tasks and duties to capable people. Yes, there will be times when you misjudge an individual or when an individual will let you down, but generally, people will rise to your expectations.

There are times, in smaller schools and school districts, when there is not enough assistance and the administrator must become jack-of-all trades. For example, in a smaller district, a superintendent may find it necessary to serve as the curriculum director, budget officer and human resources manager. However, as schools and districts increase in size, the human resources pool tends to grow. A sign of a good leader, to paraphrase Jim Collins, is "to have the right people on the bus and then make certain they are in the right seats" (Collins, 2001). The leader must also be willing to share responsibility when assistance is available.

Some administrators fail because they are unable or unwilling to share responsibilities and decision-making authority with those in their organizations. When the author was an instructional director in a fairly large school district in the Midwest, his primary job was to monitor, supervise, and evaluate the district's twenty-seven building principals. A vast majority of these principals were excellent, but the principal of the very smallest elementary school, with less than three hundred students, had difficulty sharing responsibility with others in her building. She was so concerned about her accountability for all aspects of success in her building she tried to do everything herself, including handling her secretary's clerical duties. Over a period of two or three years, the author became more insistent in our evaluative meetings that she needed to focus on what was important, rather than focusing on everything. When the principal found this impossible to do, she was reassigned back to the classroom.

When one has the ability, and perhaps the luxury, of involving others in the organization in decision making, it is possible to substantially strengthen that organization. Those to whom the leader delegates decision-making authority need to know how much latitude they have in addressing issues. They also need to know the leader will back them when they make the difficult decisions. If the leader continually second-guesses or countermands subordinates, the power of shared decision making will soon dwindle. Does this mean that anything goes with shared decision making? No, it does not mean that decisions are never examined or questioned. To borrow an old cold war phrase, the leader should "trust, but verify."

Another way to maintain accountability among decision-making subordinates is to establish goals in this area as part of an annual goal-setting conference. Leaders cannot anticipate every decision or type of decision that those under their supervision will make or encounter. However, they can establish a mechanism for examining the decision-making processes utilized and the quality of the decisions made on a regularly scheduled basis. These goal-review sessions can be used as an opportunity to provide staff development pertaining to the decision-making process. Since the research indicates that many administrators did not receive sufficient training in this area in their university preparation programs, it is incumbent upon supervisors to provide this training in the field.

GOOD VERSUS BAD CONFLICT

The media often discusses the merits of good versus bad cholesterol. Numerous authors have argued we also have good versus bad conflict. Mooney, Holahan, and Amason (2007) describe conflict as either cognitive or affective. Cognitive conflict is perceived to be a constructive contributor to the decision-making process because it reflects a group process in which participants debate and discuss alternative solutions and remedies to situations. Differing points of view can be brought forward and considered in an open environment. Theoretically, this not only brings about effective decisions, but this approach may lead to higher levels of group acceptance when the decision is actually implemented.

During the author's administrative career, he knew that it might often have been more efficient to unilaterally make a decision, but allowing often cumbersome group processes to play out almost inevitably led to more effective solutions. Administrators need to keep the end goal in mind. If we are going to Chicago, we know there are many roads leading to Chicago. As long as we reach the final destination, we should be happy as administrators. When those under our supervision are able to choose their own paths to the final destination, they are likely to be happier with the journey and the end result.

Affective conflict is conflict that becomes personal if not effectively managed by the administrator. This type of conflict occurs when personalities collide during discussions, and emotions are allowed to get out of hand. Such conflict may be driven by individual agendas, personal perspectives, competition, or perceived sanctions or rewards. This often leads to personality conflicts and perhaps the establishment of coalitions within the main decision-making group and can also lead to a lower level of acceptance of the final decision within the group, or may even lead to the inability of the group to make a decision (Jehn, 1995). As the affective conflict within a group grows, it tends to diminish the degree of cognitive conflict utilized. It takes a skilled administrative group facilitator to keep cognitive conflict from becoming affective conflict and once that genie is out of the bottle, it is hard to put it back.

Of course, many administrators use a variety of decision-making skills, including conflict resolution. Much of this is situational and usually depends on the time available for the process and the type of decision to be made. Naturally, some administrators utilize a consensus-building process with some frequency while others seldom utilize this type of process. Think of it as a continuum, with administrators scattered from one end to the other. It is likely that administrators change over time, moving along the continuum, and throughout their careers they may vary the types of decision-making processes they utilize. Most administrators learn from their experiences and become more effective in the use of particular techniques of decision making.

TYPES AND SOURCES OF CONFLICTS

The types and sources of conflicts faced by administrators vary, both in frequency and intensity. There is little doubt at the building level, many of the conflicts faced by administrators concern students. These student-related conflicts may be student-student, student-teacher, or student-administrator conflicts. In a study conducted by Anderson (2007), 119 building-level administrators responded to a series of questions regarding conflict. Ninety-two percent of the respondents indicated they encountered student-related conflict on a routine or somewhat regular basis (p. 7).

The frequency with which building-level administrators deal with student conflicts also varies according to each building's organizational structure. In some settings, an assistant principal or assistant principals may deal with most of the student discipline issues. In other settings, it may be a dean of students. There are also situations, often in smaller schools, in which the principal is the sole disciplinarian. In yet other settings, the discipline cases may be distributed among all administrators. Regardless of the organizational structure, it is likely that most building-level administrators will deal with their share of student conflict.

Also at the building level, conflict with parents is inevitable. While not quite as frequent as student conflict, most administrators deal with more than their share of conflict with parents and guardians. In the study just mentioned regarding student conflict, 86 percent of building-level administrators also volunteered that they routinely or somewhat regularly encountered conflict when dealing with parents (Anderson, 2000, p. 7). For some administrators, conflict with parents is more difficult to handle because parents are adults and seem to be on a more equal power plane with administrators than are students. Some administrators have great difficulty in their interactions with angry parents. If the parents have special needs children, the situation is often exacerbated by the family's use of an advocate.

Just over half of the administrators in the Anderson study (2007, p. 8) reported routine or regular conflicts with teachers, and only about 12 percent identified conflict with supervisors as occurring routinely or regularly (p. 8). Disputes and conflicts between administrators and teachers is not a new phenomenon. Many negotiated agreements also allow the teacher to be accompanied by a union representative during discussions involving conflicts. It is likely that the amount of conflict between building-level administrators and teachers will increase in those states that have added or will soon add legislation mandating that at least a portion of the teacher's evaluation must be based upon the academic achievement of their students. Principals and other teacher evaluators will be expected to implement the provisions of this legislation into their evaluation procedures.

Not addressed in the Anderson study were other types of conflicts that building-level administrators might face. Among these would be conflicts with constituents and members of the public who are not parents. Examples might be community leaders, governmental officials, union officials, school board members, attorneys representing students and parents, and the media. Another category of potential conflict would be other school administrators, either within or outside the district, and other district administrators not in a line relationship to the building administrator. The potential for conflict is quite broad.

The locus of conflict for administrators begins to shift as one moves out of the building and into the district office. Central-office administrators, particularly superintendents, have relatively few direct conflicts with students. Student conflicts at the superintendent level most frequently transpire at an appeal level or perhaps in an expulsion hearing. This is true, even in smaller districts, unless the superintendent plays the role of superintendent/principal. However, central-office administrators do deal with parental conflict. This happens as a result of parents' dissatisfaction with how situations involving their children were dealt with at the building level; or some parents may skip that step and jump immediately to the central office. The larger the district, the more administrators there are to help deflect some of the parental conflict away from the superintendent.

Clearly, central-office administrators deal frequently with employee conflicts, both certified and classified. It is amazing in a field dealing with human beings how many conflicts arise. Conflicts with teachers have a way of rising to the superintendent's level, particularly in smaller districts. In many districts, conflicts involving support or classified staff may even be more frequent, but may not be as intense as those involving teachers and other administrators. Often, the support staff issues involve working conditions, pay, and such, and may not be as emotionally charged as some of the more philosophical issues involving certificated staff.

Conflicts also arise between central-office and building-level administrators in both informal and formal situations. For example, a superintendent or instructional director may not be pleased with the general quality of the decisions being made by building principals, or may not feel a particular building administrator is following the district's strategic plan. Building principals may also slip into conflict situations with their bosses over the inability or refusal to follow through on district office directives. Steady complaints from those under a building leader's supervision may also lead to conflict between that principal and the district office administration. More formal conflict may arise as a result of disagreements during the formal evaluation process involving the principal or building leader. Such conflict may arise at the beginning of the process, when the district-office administrator and building-level administrator are establishing annual goals and expectations, or it may occur during other formative or summative evaluative conferences.

One issue likely to exacerbate the level of conflict between superintendents and principals is the new requirement in several states that at least a portion of the principal's evaluation must be based upon the level of student academic achievement within the principal's building. This is related to the legislation previously mentioned requiring that a portion of teachers' evaluations must now be based upon the academic performance of their students in some states. Typically, this type of legislation was passed by states hoping to receive funding through the federal RTTT program. This is one more item adding to the level of stress faced by building-level administrators. Increased stress often leads to conflict with others.

Conflict may also arise between the superintendent and other district-level administrators. The conflict involving the superintendent and other district-office personnel often is similar to the conflict between the superintendent and building-level administrators. The superintendent's district-office subordinates may not be achieving their goals, may not be following the district's strategic plan or may be making poor decisions. In some cases, a new superintendent may have inherited a district-office staff and may not be comfortable with some of those individuals. Regardless, it soon becomes evident to those throughout the district that such conflicts exist.

Intra-office conflicts may also become an issue at the district-office level. Conflicts may arise due to philosophical differences, overlapping lines of authority leading to turf issues, and so on. Petty jealousies may lead to major conflicts. Some district-office staff may feel other colleagues are "favored" by the boss. Of course, because the smooth functioning of the district office is ultimately the responsibility of the superintendent, this can pull the superintendent into another area of conflict. One of the primary tasks of any superintendent is to ensure the administrative team is a cohesive and focused group with the district's agenda in mind and at the forefront.

The most dangerous conflict for any superintendent is conflict with the board of education, and such conflict may arise for a myriad of reasons. Often, when a new superintendent joins a district, things are copasetic with the board of education. After all, the new superintendent is the board's choice. Hopefully, the new superintendent is able to be employed on a unanimous vote, which initially serves as a temporary cushion against conflict. The honeymoon for the superintendent is longer in some districts than in others. Perhaps the key factor to be considered by any superintendent candidate considering a particular school district is whether that district is a match for the superintendent's skills, beliefs, and temperament. To the extent the superintendent and the board of education are in alignment, the tenure is likely to have less conflict in the near term, at least.

In the era of the Internet, it is possible for administrative candidates to learn much about potential employing school districts before even deciding whether to apply for a particular position. At the present time, there are typically a fair number of superintendent openings available. As a former superintendent and current professor of educational administration, the author tells students to be choosy when considering moving into the superintendency because there is no need to take the first available position if it is not a match for the candidate. There is much to learn about a district and a board of education through research and contacts with other area administrators. There is also very new research coming out regarding the impact that the gender of board members has on the priorities of school districts (Hunt, Kim, Watkins, & Tripses, 2013). The same research also addresses differing district priorities according to whether a district is suburban or rural. Candidates should ponder all of these factors as they consider school districts.

Finally, superintendents may become embroiled in conflicts with other community groups and organizations, other municipal governmental agencies, and special interest groups. Occasionally, boards of education in dual district situations will become involved in conflict situations. To the extent possible, it is best to avoid conflict with the city government and police agencies, in particular. At times, this is not possible, often due to firmly held beliefs by the board of education. In such cases, the best the superintendent can do is to attempt to manage the scope and impact of such conflict.

CONFLICT RESOLUTION STRATEGIES

There are skills, strategies, and specific approaches administrators use to attempt to resolve conflict, and the strategies employed by administrators in conflict resolution depend, in part, upon the particular leadership style of each administrator. Many authors have written about transactional and transformational leadership and while transformational leadership is often touted as the more progressive or creative model, this may or may not be true regarding conflict resolution. This relates back, to some extent, to cognitive and affective conflict. A transactional leader, by definition, provides contingent rewards for reaching designated performance levels. When dealing with decision-making tasks that are not routine, transactional leaders can be directive and set boundaries and clarify roles. Such leaders can also provide feedback and rewards and can help ensure that group interactions remain positive (House, 1996).

While transactional leaders can lay the groundwork to implement and utilize cognitive conflict, transformational leaders are likely to stimulate higher levels of cognitive conflict (Kotlyar & Karakowsky, 2006). Transformational leaders do this by encouraging group members to engage in behaviors that demonstrate a personal commitment to the goals and values that the leader promotes. The group members may soon have their self-concepts engaged in a manner that is aligned with the group leader's mission (Kotlyar & Karakowsky, 2006, p. 382). Although transformational leaders may be more skilled at encouraging cognitive conflict within a group, these same leaders may have more difficulty reducing the concomitant affective conflict which may arise through the intensified group dynamics. In other words, they may have more difficulty in "talking the group down" even if they are so inclined.

The actions employed by transactional leaders may be more successful in controlling and reducing the presence of affective conflict in group situations. Such leaders often manage expectations and promote rules of conduct during group activities. These actions may help reduce frustration levels among group participants. A good transactional leader can help group members understand why their feelings are so intense and help them channel their energy in a constructive direction. Conversely, because groups led by transformational leaders are more likely to have their self-concepts involved in the decision-making process, affective conflict may increase in the attempt to salve damaged egos.

Another way of comparing transformational and transactional leadership is to understand that transformational leaders have greater potential for generating both functional (cognitive) and dysfunctional (affective) conflict within groups. In other words, such leadership can present a double-edged sword (Kotlyar & Karakowsky, 2006, p. 397). Transactional leaders tend to operate within a narrower range. It may be that the more effective leadership style for reducing negative conflict is transactional leadership, which may sound counterintuitive, since transactional leadership is most often equated with more traditional leadership, which may have a negative connotation. However, skilled transactional leaders can have a calming influence in a conflict situation.

During a public school administrative career spanning approximately a quarter of a century, the author worked with and supervised approximately fifty principals. He found that when faced with conflict, principals tended to take one of three primary paths. A small number attempted to avoid or ignore conflict at almost any cost because they simply did not like confrontation and hoped if they waited long enough, the problem would go away. A second group, which was a bit larger than the first, usually attempted to control or manage the conflict. They were forceful in their approach to conflict and tried to control the situation from the top down, often with little assistance from others. The final group, which was the largest group, genuinely worked to find solutions to conflict, engaging those involved in the conflict in the process. The principals in the group seeking solutions used different methods, with varying degrees of success.

Superintendents and other district-office administrators generally follow the same three approaches as principals as they tackle conflict in their organizations. It should be said that it is difficult for any superintendent to successfully deal with conflict through avoidance or nonconfrontation for any length of time. Most boards of education soon become disenchanted with this approach to leadership. There are some superintendents and other district-office administrators out there still relying upon the use of control to address conflict and while this is considered "old school" by many, this approach seems to work for some forceful individuals. Some boards of education prefer this approach, which leads to the perception, at least, that things in the district are running smoothly. Finally, there is a third group of superintendents and district-office administrators who attempt to find solutions and resolution to conflict as their primary approach.

In actual fact, most administrators utilize a combination of these approaches as they face conflict in their jobs. Which approach to initially implement depends upon a combination of experience and intuition. Intuition may often be informed by past experience. There are times when administrators run the gamut of approaches when dealing with one conflict. An administrator may initially attempt to ignore the situation. If this does not work, the next approach may be to work with others to find a solution. The final option may be to control the situation by imposing a solution.

An excellent way of improving administrative practice in conflict resolution is to encourage administrators to first understand their own dispositions and self-perceptions regarding the efficacy of various conflict resolution modes. One approach to this is to have administrators complete a self-assessment, such as the Thomas-Kilmann Conflict Mode Instrument (2007). This instrument was initially developed by Kenneth Thomas and Ralph Kilmann in the early 1970s. The premise of these authors is that individuals primarily fall into one of the following five conflict resolution modes: (1) competing, (2) collaborating, (3) compromising, (4) avoiding, and (5) accommodating. The two most basic dimensions for considering your choice in a conflict situation are assertiveness and cooperativeness.

This type of inventory is similar in concept to the learning style and personality indicators that many administrators have taken in the past. Instruments such as the Myers-Briggs Type Indicator and the Gregorc Style Delineator can give administrators an insight into what makes them tick as human beings. Theoretically, such instruments can first help administrators understand themselves and then can be used to help better understand that others may be coming from a different frame of reference. If administrators complete such assessments and then do not use that information in dealings with others, their time has probably been wasted. However, if administrators use this new knowledge to work more effectively with others, it has been time well spent.

It should be understood each of the modes for dealing with conflict have advantages and disadvantages. Administrators may choose one style over the other depending upon the situation, or based on the understanding he or she actually has choices in any situation. There may be times when administrators find it to their advantage to overrule their own base instincts when attempting to resolve a conflict and choose another available approach. It should be instructive to review the Thomas-Kilmann categories with this in mind.

The advantages of competing could include the ability to assert your position and stand up for your interests. It is also conceivable you could gain a quick victory in a situation. This could also serve as a means of self-defense, where you protect your interests and views from attack. Finally, this can give you a venue for testing your assumptions (Thomas, 2002, p. 13). Alternatively, disadvantages of competing can include strained work relations, less than optimal decisions, decreased initiative and motivation, and possible escalation or deadlock in conflict situations (Thomas, 2002, p. 14).

Collaborating in a conflict situation can lead to high-quality decisions, more learning and communication, commitment to the decision, and strengthened relationships among participants (Thomas, 2002, p. 13). However, there can also be costs to collaborating during conflicts. One of the most frequently mentioned drawbacks of collaboration is the time involved and the energy expended in this approach. It can also lead to psychological demands since participants must be open to new ideas, challenges and viewpoints. If you are not successful in this approach, you may end up offending the other party or parties in the conflict. It is also possible that others will attempt to exploit your trusting nature (Thomas, 2002, p. 14).

Compromising is a commonly used approach in conflict resolution. A prime example with which most administrators are familiar is the process that transpires during traditional collective bargaining. Compromise involves getting a deal completed with speed and relative efficiency. Many educators are familiar with this approach, particularly in bargaining, which may be an advantage. Theoretically, it can provide somewhat equal gains and losses for both sides in the dispute and it has the potential of helping maintain at least civil relationships between and among the parties to the dispute (Thomas, 2002, p. 13).

The downside to conflict resolution through compromise is that major concerns on both sides of the dispute may be compromised, leaving residual feelings of frustration. In the bargaining scenario outlined above, one or both parties may be left with issues that fester until the next bargaining opportunity. It is very difficult for some individuals, including board members, to put these feelings aside. This is often not good for the organization. It is also possible decisions reached through this process may not be of the highest quality and may gloss over major differences (Thomas, 2002, p. 14).

While it may not seem logical, there may be times when avoiding conflict situations is a viable option. This approach allows an administrator to avoid unpleasant people and topics and it may also enable the administrator to avoid spending time on low-priority items and can enable administrators to capture more time to become more prepared and to be ready to do battle on a topic (Thomas, 2002, p. 13). Conversely, avoidance as a conflict strategy seems to have many downsides. It is likely that some level of important work is not being done and at least a few people in the organization will be resentful their concerns are not being addressed. Avoidance implies delay and this typically leads to increased frustration within the organization. It also has a dampening impact on communications within the organization (Thomas, 2002, p. 14).

On the surface, the final mode of conflict resolution, accommodation, may seem to be the preferred method. When an administrator accommodates, he or she meets people's needs and supports them in some fashion. Accommodation is often a means of restoring harmony within the organization and can be a way of building social capital for the accommodating administrator; it is also a way of quickly ending a situation (Thomas, 2002, p. 13). Things are not always as they seem, however, and if an administrator accommodates too frequently, his or her own views are sacrificed, which can ultimately have an impact on self-efficacy. Too much accommodation can lead to a loss of respect for the leader by the troops; this may come to be seen as a sign of weakness. Finally, if an administrator accommodates too frequently, it can lead to a decrease in enthusiasm and excitement about the job (Thomas, 2002, p. 14).

ANOTHER SET OF EYES

Public school administration can be a very lonely profession. While this is true to some extent at all levels, it is especially true in the superintendency. Where principals often have other principals they can use as sounding boards, this is not true for the chief executive officers of school districts. If a superintendent is fortunate, he or she may have a good assistant or associate superintendent as a confidant. However, this is not always the case. There is a danger in always making decisions and resolving conflict in relative isolation. An administrator may unknowingly become stuck in a rut.

Administrators at all levels today have steadily increasing levels of accountability. This comes from a number of sources including enhanced attention being directed toward student academic achievement and declining revenues, which lead to increased responsibilities for administrators at all levels. As positions are eliminated or duties are added, administrative accountability grows. Increased responsibility and more stress can lead to a deleterious effect on the quality of decision making, including conflict resolution decisions. This is one reason it is important for administrators at all levels to establish networks of fellow administrators willing to regularly help them assess their recent decisions and offer feedback.

One of the factors working against collaborative decision making is the fact many of those working in schools, or school districts, as well as the many constituents of those organizations, expect the leader to make decisions. While they often want collaboration, there are other times when they just want the leader to make the decisions in the organization. As President George W. Bush said in a Rose Garden talk, "I am the decider." It is easy for administrators to fall into the trap of believing that theirs must always be the ultimate decision in situations, and taking on a mantle of invincibility in terms of the quality of their decisions. Having an external confidant or confidants willing to give feedback is critical for all administrators. We need one or more individuals out there willing to be what one of the author's bosses once called "our best loving critics."

As previously stated, it is typically easier for principals to find such outlets than it is for those in the superintendency. In many districts, there will be more than one principal, thus giving principals a source of feedback within their own districts. It is not unusual for principals to form relationships with principals from neighboring districts. Often, such relationships are formed in graduate programs and carry over into the workplace as these individuals move into administration. Having served as an instructional director for nine years in fairly large districts, and then as a superintendent for another eleven years, one of the author's biweekly duties was to conduct administrative team meetings. Inevitably, the first few minutes of each of those meetings was a time for the principals to blow off steam and discuss decisions they had made over the previous two weeks. In one district, principals were given a half-day per month to meet independently for the same purpose in rented space provided by the school district.

As a superintendent, the author always felt an obligation to address decision-making mistakes with those under his supervision. This was done to protect them rather than to hurt them. If the author believed that some of their mistakes had put them in jeopardy with the board of education, he wanted them to know as soon as possible. Having said this, feedback from their peers is more likely to have an even more positive impact on the behavior of principals in most situations. Another available source of assistance for principals in most states is available through their state's principal association.

At the superintendent level, the best source of feedback comes from other superintendents. Superintendents are almost inevitably willing to assist their peers in any way possible. The author always found this to be true, and conveyed this message to the superintendent candidates he taught over the past several years in graduate educational administration programs. While a superintendent may have a trusted assistant as a confidant, there is no substitute for talking with another individual in a similar situation. Of course, when pondering a major decision in a conflict situation, it is better to seek advice before the decision has been made rather than afterward. New superintendents should aggressively seek mentors, if they do not already have at least one individual serving in that capacity. Some states have mentoring programs for new administrators.

Illinois is one state that is experimenting with another approach to superintendent mentoring. The state superintendent organization, the Illinois Association of School Administrators (IASA), has established three field services directors with a primary responsibility for mentoring new superintendents. Each of these field services directors is a retired school superintendent. While this is a start, Illinois is a large state with over eight hundred sixty school districts, so these field services directors can only devote limited time to each of the many new superintendents in Illinois each year. However, it is possible for these field services directors to recommend potential mentors for new superintendents from among the active superintendent ranks. This program is currently funded by the IASA through member dues, since the state has eliminated all previously authorized funding for administrative mentoring programs.

ADMINISTRATIVE TRAINING NEEDS IN CONFLICT RESOLUTION

There is little doubt administrative training programs need to intensify their efforts regarding the amount and quality of curriculum devoted to decision making and conflict resolution. In a nationwide study by Foley and Lewis (1999), secondary school principals rated their skills in conflict management, negotiation, and interpersonal problem-solving skills among the five lowest items. There is little in the literature to suggest this has substantially changed since that time. In fact, research published in 2011 by Hunt, Watkins, Kersten, and Tripses confirmed that school superintendents in Illinois felt there had been a dearth of such training in their superintendent preparation programs. This is ironic in view of the fact that administrators face conflict daily.

What types of changes are needed vis-à-vis conflict resolution skills? During the first week of the author's first principalship, he engaged in a conversation with his superintendent. The superintendent asked how things were going and the author said, fine, but that he still had a lot to learn about procedures, paperwork, and so forth. The superintendent replied that those things would come with time. He went on to say, "How you deal with people is much more important to me. Your people skills are what will make or break you as an administrator."

Of course, the superintendent was correct. Unfortunately, the author had to learn those skills through on-the-job training as a building- and district-level administrator. Very little of that type of training had been included in the author's administrative training programs. Most of the coursework was filled with theory, and even though some of the professors had been successful building- and school-district administrators not much was said about the human relations skills the author would soon need in the job.

A large degree of the accountability for ensuring public school administrators have the requisite conflict resolution skills necessary in order to be successful in their administrative roles falls upon university preparation programs. Candidates need to gain a strong theoretical background in their craft, but theory alone is not enough. Conversely, they need more than "war stories" told by their regular professors or adjunct professors. A blend of theory and application should be the desired outcome of a preparation program. Those in charge of university preparation programs must be informed conflict resolution and decision-making skills both need to be taught in their programs.

Moving from a university administrative preparation program into an administrative position is somewhat analogous to moving from student teaching into teaching; some things are just more intense in the real job. However, much more can and should be done in administrative preparation programs to prepare prospective administrators for the situations they are likely to encounter in their administrative positions. According to the superintendent respondents in the previously mentioned 2011 research by Hunt, Watkins, Kersten, and Tripses, programs should rely much more heavily on case studies and role playing. Another recommendation was that the professional internships should be much more intense. In fact, none of the respondents in the statewide survey of superintendents that was conducted in 2011 said their internship was too difficult or intense.

It is entirely possible for university programs to offer such training within the coursework and structure under which they presently operate. For example, the author frequently teaches a school and community relations course in the superintendent preparation program at his university. One of the activities the students universally find to be the most helpful is that of mock interviews with the media. The author gives students a conflict-filled situation and then allows them five minutes, as superintendent, to prepare for a live interview with the media. The rest of the class acts as the media. We video-tape these interviews, and then play them back to the "superintendent" and the rest of the class. The author employs a case study approach in many of his classes, often pitting one group of students against another.

What about those administrators already in the field? Many states have a professional development requirement for the maintenance or renewal of administrators' certification. This requirement is frequently handled through an administrative academy approach in Illinois. Conflict resolution strategies could be easily taught in such workshops. Indeed, collective bargaining workshops are already frequently offered in such settings; offering many of the components involved in conflict resolution.

A VOICE OF EXPERIENCE

Far more administrators lose their positions due to conflicts with others rather than having insufficient technical skills to do the job. When the author entered his second superintendency, he followed an individual who had great educational ideas. That administrator had the potential to be a great superintendent. However, he just could not get along with people, including the board of education. At least one area superintendent attempted to counsel him regarding this trait, but this superintendent just could not help himself. When entering a new position, it is much easier to fill small shoes than large ones.

There are times when bad things happen to good people. A very competent individual followed the author when he retired from his last superintendency. The new superintendent had the misfortune of having a teacher he had dismissed in another school district as a resident in his new district. She ran for the board of education, and won. She subsequently encouraged a couple of friends to run for the board, and they also won. Soon, the superintendent was looking for another position. Fortunately, he landed in a great school district, but that does not always happen.

Many of the wounds suffered by school administrators are self-inflicted. Through excellent training and sufficient mentoring, such wounds could be avoided. The insufficiency of training that currently exists in educational administration programs was addressed earlier in this chapter. When an administrator feels himself or herself being sucked into a confrontational situation, it is often best to seek outside counsel or advice from a fellow administrator or other trusted colleague before allowing the situation to escalate out of control. Another set of eyes is almost always helpful.

Preemptive behavior may be one of the best methods of avoiding or forestalling major conflict as an administrator. In other words, selecting the right position from the beginning can reduce headaches later. The author always counsels educational administration students to fully investigate a position and a school district before even making application for a position. This is much easier, in the era of the Internet, than it was in earlier times. Administrators should be aware of their own dispositions and determine how well those align with expectations of those in charge of the district under consideration. Unless an individual is desperate for a position, it is better to wait for the right one to come along. Of course, the best time to look for a job is when you already have a good job if that is possible.

SUMMARY

This chapter began with the assertion that educational administrators are faced with a myriad of situations requiring decisions daily. Although decision making through consensus is viewed in a positive manner in the field and is often touted as a desired attribute for administrative applicants, there are many forces calling for immediate decisions. Collaborative decision making is often a time-consuming process. There are times when a top-down decision is called for in a situation. Administrators often use a variety of decision-making techniques.

Different types of decisions may call for differing decision-making processes. Some decisions, such as emergency situations, require immediate action, leaving little or no time for consultation within the organization. Other decisions that are of low impact to the organization can also be made unilaterally. However, there are times when it is appropriate for leaders to consult and collaborate with others in the organization in order to resolve a conflict or situation. While this approach may be less efficient in terms of time, it is almost always more effective vis-à-vis employee and constituent acceptance.

It is also important to consider the rationale, impact, and support for your administrative decisions. It is always wise to look up in the organization for rationale, look horizontally for impact, and look down for support. If any of these elements are missing, then your decision may be faulty and short-lived. A common administrative mistake is to make decisions that may have a negative impact on other schools or departments within a district. Administrators also need to know their decisions are in alignment with their leaders' goals and that they have the support of their troops.

There is a field of thought that says organizations can thrive on the right amount and degree of conflict. Some authors have described conflict as either cognitive conflict, which is perceived to be helpful, or affective conflict, which can be potentially destructive. While all types of leaders may attempt to promote decision making through the use of cognitive conflict, this may soon evolve into affective conflict if not handled appropriately by the leader. It appears transactional leaders, often considered more traditional, may manage conflict better during decision making than do transformational leaders. Transformational leaders typically encourage those under their supervision to become emotionally involved in the organization's goals and objectives. When and if these employees do not get their way, they may become emotionally upset.

Administrators at all levels need to be aware of their own preferred modes of conflict resolution. This will help them assess how to handle a conflict and will also give them insight into the thinking processes of others, with whom they may be working to resolve the conflict. One approach to this is for administrators to complete an assessment such as the Thomas-Kilmann Conflict Mode Instrument, which asserts that individuals primarily rely upon one of the following five conflict resolution modes: (1) competing, (2) collaborating, (3) compromising, (4) avoiding, or (5) accommodating. Regardless of the model selected, having a sense of self in conflict resolution will give an administrator an advantage. Unfortunately, many educational administrators are unaware of their own preferences vis-à-vis conflict resolution.

The chapter concluded with the claim conflict resolution and decision making are addressed far too infrequently in university-level administrative training programs. This has consistently been borne out by research in this area. It was suggested, based on feedback from superintendents and school board presidents, that programs should make much greater use of case studies, role playing, and intensified internship experiences. Administrators already in the field should be provided staff development in conflict resolution through administrative academies and other recertification activities. Conflicts arise daily in school organizations and administrators must be prepared to take accountability for handling these situations in the most effective manner possible.

FIVE

Listening Skills: The Administrator's Best Friend

Earlier in the book the author said more administrators lose their jobs over the level of their "people skills" than their technical abilities. High among the people skills required of administrators are their listening skills. Konnert and Augenstein (1990) state communication is involved in 90 percent of a superintendent's work time (p. 151). Narrowing this down further, research says listening is a key component to administrative success. Listening is critical if administrators and employees are to convert information into action plans. One study (Maes, Weldy, & Icenogle, 1997) showed managers rated listening skills and following instructions as the two very top skills contributing to their success. Haas and Arnold (1995) found listening constitutes about one-third of the traits coworkers believe are necessary to be a competent communicator.

Listening skills are not normally taught in educational administration programs, in spite of their importance in the field. It is assumed by many that such skills are either innate or that they will naturally develop as administrators progress in their careers. While there may be an element of truth to both statements, many experts now believe listening skills can be successfully taught and learned. Since research and common sense both indicate listening skills are important to the success of educational administrators, these skills should be regularly taught. This must be done both in preparation programs and in staff development situations for practicing administrators.

Some may ask why listening skills are so important, particularly if the leader has a vision and knows where he or she wants to lead the people in the organization. Those operating with a top-down mentality may fail to see the importance of listening skills and may consider the enhancement of those skills to be a waste of time. There are also individuals who believe hearing is the same thing as listening, which is not correct. One study (Brownell, 1990, p. 412) showed the poorest listening managers, as rated by their employees, rated themselves very highly as good listeners. This appears to be another case of not knowing what you do not know. It also begs the question of whether these managers were that far off on all aspects of their own abilities.

Additional research addressed later in this chapter strongly indicates men and women listen differently. Generally, women probably possess better listening skills than men. This can have many implications for those seeking positions, administrators in the field, and school districts and boards of education responsible for hiring administrators. Another interesting question to ponder is whether one typically listens differently, or more intently, to a superior than to a subordinate. That issue is also addressed in this chapter.

WHY LISTENING IS IMPORTANT

Today's environment for the superintendent is rarely predictable or smooth. Gone are the days when a superintendent could easily anticipate his or her daily activities and when that superintendent could assume few things would radically or rapidly change in the school district. Also gone, in most locations, is the scenario where the board of education can be expected to rubber stamp the recommendations of the superintendent. The same is also true for other administrators at every level in public education. Many constituents feel much more empowered and entitled to speak up than was the case in the past.

While this has changed for many reasons, the increased public desire for accountability has been the driving force. Few school districts are free from some type of reform movement. Most of these are focused on student achievement. An exacerbating force in some school districts is the rapidly changing demographic situation. Not only are some districts seeing substantial increases in the percent of African American and/or Latina/o students, but many are seeing a phenomenal increase in the number of languages spoken by the students in their districts. While some districts have had a fairly long history of educating African American and Latina/o students, some would say unsuccessfully, how do we deal with a situation in which sixty different languages are spoken by the children of a school district?

Historically, minority and immigrant families and communities have been marginalized in many school districts, but as these constituents become the majority, and as they become more politically astute, they become a force to be reckoned with. This is not said in a negative fashion. As administrators, we must recognize the world is changing and that our clientele is changing. When the author first became a principal, his building was 75 percent minority, the district was approximately 60 percent minority and the board of education was totally white. Today, although the demographics in that district have become less white, the board of education is totally African American. This has happened in just over thirty years, and such changes are happening much more rapidly in many communities. Whether an administrator is Caucasian, African American, Latina/o, Asian, or from another ethnic group, it is wise to pay attention to the shifting demographics of the school district.

The drop in income levels in many districts has been significant, particularly as related to the recession of 2008–2009. What were once middle-class schools with a small free- and reduced-lunch count are now lower-income, with 60 to 70 percent of their students eligible for these services. Many families are struggling, and a large proportion of parents in some locations may be unemployed, underemployed, or perhaps working two or three jobs to make ends meet. Such parents may not have the time or energy to devote to school activities, meetings at the school, and so on. This makes it even more critical for administrators to reach out to families.

Administrators must also address other constituencies in today's public education environment. In some communities, parents from conservative religious groups may resist the introduction of any type of values education into the curriculum. Historically, when parents objected to a particular curricular unit, administrators would typically excuse that child from the activity and provide a meaningful alternative activity. Often, school districts would have formal policies permitting parents to challenge specific curricular issues. The public essentially abided by a live-and-let-live mentality in this arena. Today, it has become more typical for parents to say that not only is a particular unit not appropriate for their own children, but it should not be offered to any child.

Much more common today are disagreements with parents of disabled children. While a large proportion of such parents work very positively with their schools and school districts, a few engage in disputes with their schools and districts on a regular basis. For whatever reason, some parents get off on the wrong foot with the educators in their children's schools and then become distrustful of all educators and all recommendations proposed by the school or districts. At times, the situation escalates even further when the parents bring an advocate into the situation. This action often hardens the stance of the educators, and soon the adults seem to forget they may need to compromise to meet the needs of the child in the situation.

Another cause of conflict and probable cause of disagreement between administrators and constituents is the generally poor fiscal situation in many states and, hence, among many school districts. Whether it is the elimination of talented and gifted programs, student activities, or a reduction in teaching staff in general, conflicts may arise with either parents or employees. Taxpayers, in general, seem to be much more resistant to tax increases for educational purposes, even in relatively wealthy suburban districts. While it has never been easy to pass an operational fund increase in most districts, it has become virtually impossible in some locations. This is a real change in some wealthier suburban districts.

A final area of growing conflict is the increased high-stakes nature of teacher and principal evaluation in many states. As already addressed earlier in the book, the rush of many states to enhance their chances of RTTT funding has led several states to tie at least a portion of teacher evaluation to improvements in student academic performance. The same is true for principal evaluation in some states. In some states, these new rules have made it a bit easier for administrators to successfully dismiss weak teachers. In other states, seniority is no longer the primary or first factor to consider when implementing reduction-in-force mandates from the board of education.

The author taught school law in the principal preparation program at his university for several years, and one of our major exercises dealt with teacher evaluation. Prior to RTTT, a large proportion of the public school teachers in these classes described the teacher evaluation systems in their districts as a "joke." They no longer describe these systems in the same fashion. Now that 30 to 50 percent of a teacher's evaluation is based on how well their students perform academically, the communication between teachers and their evaluators becomes even more important. The same can be said for communications between principals and their evaluators, since increasing numbers of principals are now being at least partially evaluated on student academic performance.

The issues outlined above are not the only issues facing building-level and district administrators today. However, all of the issues listed above have either emerged or become more intense over the past generation, making the role of educational administrator more difficult. All of these situations can be made a bit more manageable through the implementation of enhanced listening skills by building- and district-level administrators. The messages received by today's administrators are both ambiguous in some situations and contradictory in others. All of these situations relate directly to administrative accountability and to the degree to which administrators meet these demands successfully. Enhancing listening skills is one way to improve accountability. First, however, what are listening skills?

WHAT IS LISTENING?

The question should be what is effective listening? Most researchers believe that it is both a cognitive and behavioral action. In other words, it contains active elements if implemented or conducted effectively. Listening is the first communication skill learned in infancy, and this skill continues to develop into the secondary school years. One study (Brownell, 1990) even indicates listening skills may decline after a certain age (forty-five in this particular study).

Several definitions and models of listening have been advanced over the years, and while these typically contain between three and six elements, most contain active and passive listening as two of those elements. Both active and passive traits are probably required in order to be a good listener, but too much of either can also be negative, depending on the situation. Some researchers have added the element of empathy to listening and one group (Drollinger, Comer, & Warrington, 2006) talks about active empathic listening. In this scenario, the listener must sense, process and respond to what is being said in order to properly receive the message. Sensing includes more than simply hearing; it also involves picking up on nonverbal clues such as body language and facial expressions being provided by the talker. Sometimes these messages are only implied, and the listener must process what the speaker is saying and separate the wheat from the chaff.

When processing information, the listener must first understand what is being said. The listener must also analyze the implications of what is being stated by the speaker. Concurrently, the listener must evaluate the importance of the cues being sent and must subsequently remember the message for future use. Clearly, some administrators are better at this than others. Picking up on the appropriate cues can be a nuanced activity.

Responding back to the speaker is the final dimension of active listening. The manner in which this response is returned may be the difference between just active listening and active and empathetic listening. When a listener responds, signals are sent back to the speaker indicating that the speaker has been heard. Responses can be both verbal and nonverbal. The listener can give the speaker such cues as a variety of facial expressions or head nods, or may give the speaker a series of verbal prompts. Occasionally, this may lead to clarifying questions on the part of the listener.

Another group of researchers (Barker, Pearce, & Johnson, 1992) talked about four listening types: active, involved, passive, and detached. It was their conclusion the active listener would be the most effective. Active listeners are energetic and focused in their communication exchanges. Next in the continuum of effectiveness would be the involved listener. Involved listeners attempt to at least receive and reflect upon the message being communicated, but they may not effectively respond to the speaker. The passive listener deflects responsibility for the communication back to the speaker, and the detached listener, perceived to be the least effective, withdraws and does not truly participate in the conversation.

Yet another approach, suggested by Brownell (1990) is what she calls the HURIER Model of listening behaviors. HURIER is an acronym for hearing, understanding, interpreting, evaluating, remembering, and responding. Brownell suggests while these elements of listening behaviors are interrelated, they are actually separate skill areas, which can then be addressed for training purposes. The particular model of listening ascribed to by an administrator is probably not as important as understanding the importance of listening and that listening is more than hearing. Administrators should also know the importance of active listening as well as the likely effectiveness of empathetic listening. Administrators should also know listening skills can be learned, practiced, and improved. Both building-level and district administrators must also assess their own motives in utilizing listening skills.

IMPROVEMENT OF LISTENING SKILLS

Some administrators use listening skills to control or manipulate a situation, while others listen with a more open mind and are willing to be influenced by what they hear. The first type of administrator typically has some type of agenda he or she wishes to promote, and uses listening skills in order to better promote that agenda. While these administrators may appear to be empathetic listeners, they primarily generate such feelings in order to better understand what motivates the speaker. The author does not place a value judgment on such tactics and occasionally used them as a building-level and district administrator. However, he did not use these exclusively and frequently used listening skills to gain a better understanding of a particular individual or situation.

Focusing on the sensing, processing, and responding aspects of listening is a straightforward way of strengthening administrative listening skills. While all of these aspects are important, sensing may be the most difficult to master for many administrators. It requires being sensitive both to what the speaker is saying and not saying. It means listening to the tone of the conversation and discerning what the speaker is implying as well as stating. A key element of sensing is ascertaining the speaker's feelings and determining what is really important to the speaker including the speaker's major concerns. Intuition is important to the sensing aspect of listening, where you put yourself into the speaker's shoes.

Processing what is heard comes next. During this phase, the administrator concentrates on remembering what the speaker said; this may even entail taking notes. The listener notes the points made by the speaker and prioritizes these points, often connecting these points to those made in previous conversations in order to assess the relative importance of the speaker's issues. This phase may also require the listener to ask for clarification from the speaker on particular points. This phase requires the listener to work.

There may be some overlap between processing information during a conversation and responding to that information. In a sense, asking a speaker to clarify issues constitutes a type of response. However, the response stage is typically utilized to keep the speaker on track or to encourage a speaker to delve into more depth on a topic. It is during this stage that the listener signals he or she is receptive to the ideas being presented. The listener may ask probing or follow-up questions to show the speaker's position or assertions are understood, which may even include paraphrasing or restating of the speaker's points. Usually, when the listener asks probing questions, this tells the speaker the listener is indeed interested in the topic or position being posited.

If an administrator is aware of these phases of the listening process, then he or she can practice and improve on these skills. Active and empathetic listening can help an administrator build or strengthen relationships both inside and outside of his or her organization. Contrast this type of listening with that in which the administrator seems to be distracted or disinterested during a conversation. Indicators of such disinterest may include continuing to read a document or fiddling with a cellular phone while the other party is speaking. The speaker is quite likely to see this as disinterest rather than multitasking. Most employees and constituents really appreciate the chance to be heard and often all parents want of an administrator is to be heard and to blow off a bit of steam. Most teachers appreciate an administrator that is willing to listen, even though they know the administrator's response to a request will not always be yes.

While some individual administrators may have the ability to independently improve their listening skills, it may be preferable to enhance these skills through participation in university preparation programs or staff development workshops. Either venue can focus on both training and development. Training focuses primarily on skills and development addresses the attitudes necessary to effectively listen. In the university setting, instructors can establish role playing scenarios and case studies that give administrators practice in listening and discerning meaning from conversations. Such sessions can either be videotaped and/or evaluated by other students in the class to give feedback to participants. Such activities should be done frequently and growth should be expected among participants.

In the field, practicing administrators can receive staff development in the improvement of listening skills. This can either be done by outside facilitators, as administrators participate in administrative academies and other workshops, or can take the form of peer-assisted, self-directed learning in the field. Superintendents can help principals, directors, and others they supervise develop and enhance listening skills through mentoring, coaching, and feedback. This feedback can be both formal and informal. It can be as structured as specific job performance goals for which the administrator is held accountable or something as informal as periodic conversations about the topic of listening.

It should also be noted generational attributes may play a role in listening skills. The young educators coming forward today have been raised in a world of electronic communications, including e-mail, texting, tweeting, and so on. It is likely these influences will have an impact on the art of listening and more traditional communications in general. It may be too early to determine the exact impact on listening skills, but this generational phenomenon is something that school administrators need to keep in mind as they communicate with these younger educators and parents. The issue of whether the increased use of electronics will prove to help listening or hinder it is one that needs to be monitored and addressed.

YES, MEN AND WOMEN ARE DIFFERENT

There is research that claims that female managers are better listeners than their male counterparts (Brownell, 1990; Barker, Pearce, & Johnson, 1992). According to the study by Brownell (1990), even though women accounted for just over a third of the total management group studied, they constituted over half of the highly rated listener group. Earlier research (Buck, Miller, & Caul, 1974) indicated females are more outwardly expressive than men and they are more likely to externalize their emotions and present more evident nonverbal cues than men. The tendency of many women to demonstrate their responses through smiling, eye contact, head nodding, and other similar positive indicators undoubtedly adds to the speaker's perception of empathy and interest. Of course, there is an exception to every rule. When the author worked in a fairly large district in the Midwest, the district's chief negotiator was a woman known as the "Iron Lady"—before the epithet was given to Margaret Thatcher.

The folklore regarding the superintendency is that superintendents are talkers and to remain silent as a superintendent has been perceived as a sign of weakness by some. In a very interesting article (Brunner, 2002) female superintendents stated that sometimes when male superintendents talk, they are "just talking" (p. 424) and what they are saying is not important. Rather, the talk may just be a part of power games they are playing. These same female superintendents stated that when they spoke up in administrative meetings, they were often ignored or discounted by their male counterparts. The author has received the same type of feedback from female superintendents and other administrators in graduate administration programs. Often, these comments pertained to the female administrators' relationships with their boards of education.

It may well be the conditions facing building and district administrators today can be more effectively addressed via the types of listening skills more frequently utilized by women. Administrators work in a much more chaotic and unpredictable world than they did even fifteen years ago. It is no longer possible for an administrator to truly "control" situations through force of character or top-down methods, at least not for any length of time. Regarding listening, active empathetic listening seems to be the preferred method in today's world. Some would even say administrators need to employ proactive listening.

Historically, many superintendents used the control of information as a source of power (Kowalski, 1999). In order to protect their own personal power, superintendents often limited access to information to others in their organization. There was also a strong sense superintendents should use their personal power to promote their vision for the school district. It was felt superintendents should use their cachet to persuade or convince others to comply or agree with the superintendent's vision, and while there may seem to be an element of "father knows best" in this approach, this was the course preferred by many boards of education. The author distinctly remembers a situation during one of his last board reviews as a public school superintendent where this type of feeling was expressed. While he received a very positive review, the board made it clear that it wanted him to express his own vision and opinions more frequently and more publicly. This was during an era when he was attempting to distribute leadership more broadly.

The new approach to leadership is moving to a more distributive model, one in which the superintendent or principal is not the only one in the district or building with the vision for progress. If this is the case, what should be done differently and how should this influence listening skills? Because the world is more diverse and more complex, and this is increasingly manifested in school buildings and districts, "father knows best" or even "mother knows best" is not likely to be the most effective approach to leadership. In order to be accountable to their constituents, educational administrators must ensure that their dialogue is open and multidirectional. In other words, administrators must be truly willing to listen and to receive input from multiple constituent groups.

Because many superintendents know what they want to hear before they begin listening, this limits what those superintendents actually hear. Rather, it is suggested that educational leaders should become comfortable with contradiction and must be willing to listen to other points of view. Leaders should be willing to be informed through listening to determine what the situation is rather than always informing others regarding nearly every situation. This makes life more chaotic and unpredictable and places an entirely new spin on planning (Wheatley, 2006). It means educational leaders must be willing to appreciate dissent, which will be difficult for those administrators averse to conflict.

In one of the courses the author periodically teaches in a principal preparation program, the ethic of justice and the ethic of care are discussed. Certainly, the ethic of justice connotes a legalistic tone and is often perceived to be the more "political" approach to addressing issues. However, in our increasingly multicultural society, the ethic of care certainly must become preeminent. Women may be more naturally disposed toward the ethic of care and may have the advantage in terms of their listening skills in this area. Regardless of gender, educational leaders of our nation's public schools must be front and center in the fight for social justice. This will typically not be easy and may be contrary to what is desired by community leaders. However, nobody ever said the job would be easy.

NAVIGATING DIFFICULT SITUATIONS THROUGH LISTENING

The author served as the superintendent of three separate school districts during the last portion of his public school career. One of the statements he always made during the interview process for each of these positions was that he wanted to help establish the type of district in which a great idea was as likely to come from a kindergarten teacher as from the superintendent. Although he worked at making this happen, it cannot be said in all honesty that he ever completely met that goal. To meet that type of goal, a superintendent needs to be willing to constantly listen to what his or her employees, constituents, and bosses are saying. As much as a superintendent would like to affirm every speaker and subsequently acquiesce to every request, this is impossible due to competing needs and political forces in the district.

However, progress can be made along this road as long as speakers know they truly have a valid voice and that the administrator will occasionally agree and affirm their requests. It helps, when denying a request, if the administrator will give the speaker a reason for the denial rather than just saying no. While the speaker will probably still be disappointed by the rejection, in most cases the speaker will respect the superintendent for taking the time to give a rationale for the decision. For this to work, the administrator occasionally has to say yes. At the other extreme is the administrator who says yes too often and cannot follow through on all promises.

Listening by educational leaders is not always one-to-one and can take place in a variety of contexts. These conversations can be in either individual or group setting. Really listening to what students and parents have to say can give any administrator useful information if the administrator approaches every conversation with an open mind. Many times, conversations with students and parents involve disciplinary situations, where emotions are running high from the beginning. Often, the administrator is placed in a position of deciding whether a teacher, or perhaps an assistant principal or principal has made the right decision in a situation. Probably anyone who has been a building-level administrator has been in a situation in which the teacher made the wrong call. What should be done in this situation?

Many administrators were brought up in the tradition of covering for the teacher and then privately addressing the situation later with the teacher. Superintendents frequently do the same when a principal has made a mistake. When administrators take such actions, do they forget to whom they are primarily accountable? All administrators make mistakes, and giving individuals cover for one of these mistakes may not seem to be such a bad thing. The problem is such actions tend to become patterns of behavior. It also sends a clear message to students and parents that administrators do not sincerely listen.

The author's perception about such behavior changed forever when he joined the administrative team of a school district in Colorado Springs. When he informed some old friends who were residents of that district that he would be working there, they said, "This district is really different. They actually listen to parents and bend over backwards to accommodate parents." They were right; the culture of the district was to do everything possible to please the customer. A major part of this was listening intently and responding in a positive and respectful fashion. Administrators learned that they were expected to openly admit their mistakes.

This attitude paid off in many ways including student achievement and voter support for the school district. This was a rapidly growing school district and new schools were continually under construction. There was never a fear of a failed referendum because the parental support for the district was so high. It was not unusual for people to pay $15,000 to $20,000 more for a home just because it was within the boundaries of that particular school district. Administrators at all levels learned they could not expect to be shielded from mistakes, and this led to more sincere listening and better decisions.

The author learned a great deal during his administrative career by intently listening to the principals he supervised. He served as an instructional director for nearly a decade in three separate districts of several thousand students each where his primary role was to supervise, monitor, and evaluate principals. In one district, he annually evaluated twenty-seven principals. In that district, he used a goal-setting process as the evaluative tool. Goals would be set in September, and a midpoint evaluation would be conducted with each principal in January. After a goal progress discussion of a couple of hours, each principal received a written narrative formative evaluation of several pages. At the end of the year the same process was repeated.

While this was an incredible amount of work, it was fascinating what information was garnered during those conversations. The author learned to not only listen to what the principals said and how they said it, but also to listen for what they did not say. These formal conversations gave an indication of which buildings should receive additional supervisory attention. It soon became evident which principals were really willing to stretch themselves with their proposed goals, and which principals were trying to slide by without really challenging themselves. Some principals were willing to truly be open and honest during those conversations while others were less forthcoming. While there was seldom a sense that principals lied, it became clear some frequently omitted information. While these principals were colleagues, they still viewed the author as an individual holding power over them.

During his last two superintendencies, the author engaged in another type of listening on a regular basis, holding informal monthly meetings with the leaders of the teachers' union in his school districts. During these meetings, which typically lasted an hour or two, a variety of issues, potential problems and ways of moving the district forward were discussed. After about a year of such meetings in each district, an element of trust was developed and both parties knew they could speak openly and honestly, without fear of having conversations repeated outside the meeting. If the teachers felt a particular principal was not abiding by the spirit of the negotiated agreement, they knew that the situation would subsequently be addressed with the principal. If the author believed a teacher was behaving inappropriately in some fashion, the union leadership would do its best to bring that teacher into line.

Through this process, small problems were prevented from growing into larger problems. The fact that these meetings were held over nine years in two districts contributed to the absence of any grievances filed in those two districts over those nine years. Two interesting actions arose from these meetings in the last district. The union grievance chair and the author became friends and they and their spouses socialized on a regular basis. Second, when the author announced his retirement, the union negotiated the monthly meeting with the superintendent into the next contract so they could be assured that these meetings would continue under the new regime.

Another listening experience involving teachers, albeit in a group setting also transpired in the last two districts where the author served as superintendent. District Advisory Committees were initiated in both districts. While the primary focus of both of these committees was curricular in nature, they were structured to address any district issues of concern to teachers. While this concept is not unusual, they were structured in a fashion that would help ensure open feedback. In each district, principals were asked for recommendations for representatives from their buildings. Not only was a balanced representation selected regarding subject matter and grade levels, but the committees were not packed with "yes" people. The intent was to include at least a few contrarians in the mix.

These committees had a set agenda for each monthly meeting, and every member had the right to submit agenda items. In all honesty, few teachers took advantage of that opportunity. However, each meeting concluded with an "open forum," and the representatives did raise issues at every meeting during that section of the agenda. The administrative team found it really needed to listen during these sessions and had to be thoughtful in its responses. Sometimes the responses were immediate and on other occasions, committee members had to wait for a response, but over time they came to appreciate the fact that a response would be forthcoming.

In the last district, it was somewhat difficult to actually encourage teachers to become actively involved in the District Advisory Committee. This was because the previous superintendent had overused committees and had rarely followed through on recommendations. In other words, the perception was that he rarely listened. With the establishment of the new committees, committee members were assured that their time would be respected and that their time would not be wasted. It took the better part of a year before the committee members were convinced that the new superintendent would follow through on his claims. Once that happened, committee members became much more open during the meetings.

Two other situations involved listening to parents and other constituents in group situations. In essence, both involved what might be described as the launch of trial balloons and gauging public reaction to those potential initiatives. Of course, these situations probably ran counter to truly open listening, but both were honestly intended to gather input. The first transpired when the author was the director of the K–12 university laboratory school at the University of Northern Colorado. Staff were experimenting with what were perceived to be fairly radical organizational and curricular changes, and parental input was needed. Among the changes being suggested were the replacement of the traditional K–12 grades with five levels (I–V) and a move to a truly interdisciplinary curriculum, even at the high school level. Two public meetings for parents were conducted to outline our thinking and to receive input.

The range of emotions ran from "We didn't sign up for this," to "We trust you implicitly." What was really learned from listening was although parents had enrolled their children in an alternative, albeit technically public school, many were afraid of change. Another bit of information garnered from listening was that the concerns were greater among high school parents and students. They were upset regarding the possible impact the new course and organizational structure might have on college admissions. As the age of their children declined, the less concerned parents seemed to be in this situation.

The second trial balloon also was released in Colorado about seven years later. This experience was in Colorado Springs, as the school district was developing action goals to move the district into the next decade. The administrative team developed a set of approximately 10 tentative major goals for the school district and decided to seek public input regarding these goals. This was the district previously described as being very open to parental input. A series of public meetings, primarily for parents, were held at various schools throughout the district on different evenings, in the attempt to receive as much public input as possible.

The author conducted one of the meetings held at a high school near the center of the district. One of the major goals dealt with respecting diversity and appreciating the strengths of differing groups. While this may seem like a worthy goal, and perhaps an innocuous goal, it did not please one of the very conservative parents in the audience. He stood up, visibly red-faced and angry and shouted, "Do you mean if my son is a bigot, he cannot graduate?" What was the real message here? Of course, his real message was that he believed that the public schools have no business teaching values and should stick to teaching basic curriculum.

It also pays to listen to other constituent groups. As a superintendent, the author always worked in growing school districts, and found it necessary to work to pass a referendum in each of the three districts he served in this capacity. Listening to constituents is critical in such situations. While it is important to hear what taxpayers are saying when you take your referendum pitch (dog and pony show) on the road, speaking to various community groups, it is probably more important to listen to constituents before taking the presentation on the road. You need to assess how the community is feeling about various aspects of your referendum package.

This can be determined through community meetings, community surveys, or interviews with key individuals. In one of the author's districts, it was mandatory to hold a conversation with one of the large farmers in the district before having any chance of success on a referendum. This very conservative individual was a good person and had previously served as the president of the school board in the community. If nothing else, he at least had to agree not to openly oppose a referendum attempt. The author held a conversation with this individual and his wife in their kitchen over a cup of coffee and utilized what he heard as the referendum committee subsequently crafted its successful referendum proposal.

Another occasion when it was important to listen to a constituent group was when one of the author's districts found it necessary to consider reducing the school district's budget by approximately $2 million. To assist with this process and hopefully help mount a successful educational fund referendum, a community-based Budget Reduction Advisory Committee was organized in the district. This committee was comprised of community leaders, the president of the band parents' organization, booster club president, and others. District administrators outlined the fiscal situation to this group, and they listened. Then they developed their set of recommendations, and district administrators and board members listened. Ultimately, the members of this group were among the district's greatest advocates as it successfully passed a referendum to restore $2.2 million in cuts that had been made to balance the budget.

A major group to whom a superintendent should carefully listen is the board of education. This is addressed in greater detail in the last chapter, but one example is given here. The author found that one of the best ways to get off on a positive note in his school districts was to individually interview each of the seven school board members upon entrance into the district. This was accomplished during the first summer, before the school year actually began. This was a fairly unstructured interview, and the board members did most of the talking.

First, board members were asked to talk about themselves, their jobs, their families, their hobbies and interests. Second, they were asked to outline any concerns they had regarding the district. Finally, they were prompted to share their points of pride regarding the school district. Working with these same board members in each of the districts he served, the author found that by listening carefully during these initial interviews, his job was made easier. To a person, these board members had honestly described their feelings and priorities during those initial conversations.

LISTENING TO DIFFERENT AUDIENCES

Do administrators listen differently to different audiences? In other words, is an administrator more likely to listen to a boss than to a constituent, and is that administrator likely to employ different listening skills depending on the audience? While this may happen to some extent with certain administrators, approaches to listening are fairly solidly entrenched, and most building and district administrators tend to employ the same skills regardless of audience. At the same time, the quality of listening skills can be improved through hard work and practice, and when this happens all audiences tend to benefit from the improvement. The key is for individual administrators to understand they are the ones primarily accountable for this improvement.

There are many stories of individuals currying favor with the boss, and many have personally witnessed such situations. In these cases, the subordinate makes a great display of listening intently but often gains little new information or knowledge from such behavior. While it may bring the "listener" some amount of short-term gain, this approach is unlikely to carry an individual through a career. Ultimately, such individuals are often exposed for employing such tactics.

Other individuals do not listen to their bosses and make little effort to cover up their disdain for their employers. Earlier in the book, the author mentioned that it is easier to fill small shoes than large ones when entering a new position. In two of his superintendencies, he followed individuals who simply discounted anything said by their boards of education. They had the attitude that their own personal ideas were what would move the district forward and felt that the board had little to contribute. In both cases, this ultimately led to a split, with the majority of the board requesting the superintendents' departure from the district.

The author has also dealt with subordinates who may have heard what was said but did not really listen to the message being conveyed. It is always the chief administrator's responsibility to make it clear to those supervised where they stand with their supervisor, and perhaps more importantly, with the board of education. Two principals come to mind in this regard. While both were genuinely liked by their students, neither was very strong in dealing with teachers. Specifically, in each of these districts, the board of education had an agenda of moving the district forward. Neither board wanted to maintain the status quo.

The first principal was a high school principal and had been in that position for about a dozen years. Prior to that, he had taught in the same high school for several years. He was friends with many of the teachers and was hesitant to push them to work harder or to try new techniques. The board perceived this to be laziness. In the author's second year as superintendent, he held a long conversation with the principal, expressing his concerns, as well as those of the board. That talk proved to be ineffective.

The next year, the high school principal was given a written memorandum that clearly outlined approximately twenty specific areas of improvement needed. When this memo was delivered to the principal, each point was also verbally addressed. When it came time for a review of his progress, he had made virtually no improvements. He was reassigned to another position at mid-year. While part of his issue may have been an inability to perform at the required levels, a major part of his issue was that he truly did not listen to what was being said and did not believe the board and his supervisor were serious.

The second principal was a middle school principal who wanted to be friends with everyone and did not like any type of conflict with his staff. He found it difficult to say no to teacher requests. He had a couple of really bad actors in his building and had been directed by the board to deal with these individuals. When the author came to the district, he reiterated these calls for improvement and worked these situations into the principal's goals. This principal was a very likeable individual and thought he could talk anyone into anything and also thought that he could talk himself out of any situation.

His pattern followed a pattern similar to the first principal, and he was ultimately reassigned to another position. Lest you think the author was totally ineffective as a supervisor, these two examples are cited as exceptions. In many other cases, principals were helped to improve and turn situations around At least a fair portion of the blame in the case of the two reassigned principals was due to their poor listening skills. Looking back, it is unfortunate that this was not recognized earlier.

There will be times when administrators clearly hear what is being said by their supervisor, but disagree with what is being said. This is different from not hearing. In these situations, the administrator often has an ethical or philosophical decision to make regarding compliance. Administrators often discuss whether a particular situation is one over which he or she should "fall on their sword." In some situations, administrators may decide to comply with what their supervisor says and live to fight another day. Alternatively, an administrator may choose to stand and fight over the situation.

In conclusion, the need to listen more intently and to a wider range of audiences is now a critical skill for all building- and district-level administrators. As administrators listen to various audiences, they increasingly struggle with issues of accountability. Are they accountable primarily to their bosses or to those constituents they serve? To which particular group should an administrator be held most accountable? Should administrators attempt to even things out by implementing an ethic of justice, or should the ethic of care prevail? If an administrator at least knows he or she is facing conflicts in these areas, due to listening, that administrator is ahead of many colleagues. These issues are addressed in more detail in the last chapter of the book.

A VOICE FROM THE FIELD

In this chapter, it was reported there may be times when administrators really hear what a supervisor is saying but may choose to ignore the message due to ethical situations. When the author was about a third of the way through his administrative career, he was an instructional director in a fairly large school district in the Midwest. The primary role in that situation was the monitoring, supervision, and evaluation of twenty-seven building principals. There were many excellent principals in that district, but the one the author considered to be among the very best was the leader of the district's only magnet school. To say the least, this was a school with "demanding" parents. This principal typically handled her school, and these parents with skill and grace. Occasionally, a parent would complain to the board of education about a particular situation, but the principal was almost inevitably proven to be right in these situations.

Each year, during a closed session with the board of education, the author was asked to give an overview of his evaluations of all twenty-seven principals. Some years, the board request was to rate them as above average, average, or below average and in other years, the board wanted an A, B, C type of rating. During the author's third year with the district, he was reviewing his ratings of the principals and things were going smoothly until he addressed the magnet school principal. The author made a statement to the effect that "she is one of your best principals." The board president and another board member took real exception with this and asked whether he would reconsider his rating. He felt he could not change the recommendation on this issue and after his presentations were concluded, he was excused from the meeting.

Eventually, he learned that while most of the principals received a 5 percent raise (those were the good old days), the magnet school principal was given a 3 percent raise. Also, whereas the district office administrative staff members were also given 5 percent raises, he received a 4 percent raise. While this was not a huge financial hit on his part, the message had certainly been sent. The magnet school principal resigned from the district and enrolled in a doctoral program in educational administration. She eventually became the chair of a department of educational administration in a university and exerted a positive and progressive influence on hundreds of prospective administrators. The author also decided to leave the district after one more year. He understood it was legitimate for the board of education to disagree with his decision in this situation, but he was perhaps more upset that the superintendent and the associate superintendent did not speak up on his behalf.

This was a situation where a major concept was learned from negative modeling. Although the author still holds great respect for the superintendent and associate superintendent, he vowed that if he ever became a superintendent, he would support administrators with the board when he knew they were right. He did his best to uphold that pledge. This came into play during his first superintendency, in particular. The key in that situation was to continually encourage the board members to really listen to what their principals were saying.

SUMMARY

In this chapter, it was asserted listening skills are not sufficiently taught in most educational administration programs. The increased call for accountability has made all levels of public school administration more difficult. Consequently, the need for listening skills is now greater than ever. Rare is the building-level or district administrator who is able to control the flow of information and execute the job without receiving and utilizing input from others through the use of listening skills. Some educational administrators possess more advanced listening skills than others.

The changing demographics have also made improved listening skills more critical than ever. Not only does the nation have a much more racially and ethnically diverse society, but many districts are also facing a precipitous drop in income level among many of their constituents. There was a time in the past when such groups were discounted, either consciously or unconsciously, by administrators. That is no longer possible, and certainly not desirable. A variety of groups are now demanding a voice in how schools and school districts are being run. Administrators also face the growth of religious and political groups demanding that public schools and school districts be run according to their particular agendas.

Other issues leading to the need for enhanced listening skills are the poor fiscal conditions that have been present in the economy since 2008. An additional impetus includes the recent calls for linking teacher and principal evaluation to student achievement. This alone is likely to encourage teachers and administrators to listen more intently to one another during evaluation conferences. The poor economic conditions make taxpayers more aware of academic performance, because they want to ensure that they are receiving the very best educational value possible for each dollar spent. Educational administrators and taxpayers need to hold serious discussions and listen intently to one another to jointly find solutions to the financial crisis.

The fact listening is both cognitive and behavioral was addressed in this chapter. While several models of listening have been advanced over the years, most state listening can be either active or passive. Regarding active listening, some authors also state listening should be active and empathetic. Empathetic listening includes both verbal and nonverbal cues to the speaker. These are skills that can be enhanced through practice.

Researchers also say men and women listen differently. Women are more open to being influenced via the listening process. This may be because they are more attuned to the ethic of care, which many say is what leads to more effective leadership and better accountability for the various constituents of schools and school districts. This type of flexible and open listening can be taught in university preparation programs and in staff development programs for practicing administrators. To ignore this will do nothing to resolve the conflicts faced by administrators on a daily basis.

SIX
The Future of Administrative Accountability: Friend or Foe?

During the author's first superintendency in the mid-1990s, a particular part of his district's elementary curriculum did not align directly with the state testing system. A concept the state tested at the third-grade level was a topic the district's teachers taught during the fourth-grade year. In that era, the author felt quite comfortable telling the teachers not to worry about this issue. Because the staff had thoughtfully crafted the scope and sequence of the curriculum, he had no problem explaining the dip in scores to district parents. Less than a decade later, he would have been hard-pressed to take the same stance, due to the influence of NCLB.

This has become a difficult time to be a building-level or district administrator, which is somewhat evidenced by the dearth of good candidates for administrative positions. Every job in education, including teaching, is more difficult today than fifteen years ago. This situation has been exacerbated by public criticism and calls for increased accountability, both driven in large part by the fiscal position most states find themselves in today. When the money is not there, states are unable to address all of their priorities. This inability to meet needs leads to anger and frustration, which, in turn, leads to a search for someone to blame. In many cases, that someone has been public education.

Over the past several years, the author has taught full-time in both the principal and superintendent preparation programs of a Midwestern university. Recently, the university also added a doctoral program, which includes a number of practicing superintendents. Since the economic downturn of 2008, in particular, the negative impact of the working conditions on the university's administration students has become much more evident. Many of these administrators have been involved in cutting large numbers of teaching positions. Others have been forced to dismiss or reassign administrators, or close school buildings.

Add to this the requirement in many states to tie teacher and principal evaluation to student achievement and the stress is even higher. In Illinois, this enhanced requirement for teacher evaluation was accompanied by a state-mandated online training that required countless hours and testing during the summer of 2012. This was complicated by the poor quality of the instructional videos and the subjectivity of the training materials. Of course, the training became available at the same time when most administrators typically took their vacations. This made an already stressful situation even worse.

As instructors in educational administration programs, the author and his colleagues have found it challenging to maintain a positive focus with educational administration students in view of the current situation, often feeling more like counselors than teachers. This is a statewide phenomenon in Illinois. The author and his university colleagues meet periodically with other professors of educational administration from across the state, and the conditions are the same in all of the public and private universities preparing administrators. It would be easy to give up in what seems to always be an uphill battle, but the students in our public schools need the best teachers and administrators possible. Because they deserve the best, educational administrators must find ways to reverse the current situation and steadily improve the conditions under which students and educators learn and work. In large part, this will mean bringing about redefinitions of administrative accountability.

AN IDEAL WORLD

There are many changes that would improve the system of public education in the United States. Ironically, the nation had some of these items in the past, but let them slip away. Perhaps one of the most important things would be a return to a truly comprehensive curriculum. During the NCLB era, the curriculum has narrowed to focus primarily on those areas tested under NCLB. Many districts have also spent far too much time drilling students on test-taking skills.

A major study (Center on Education Policy, 2006) conducted about four years after the implementation of NCLB found that over 70 percent of the elementary schools in their sample had already narrowed or eliminated nontested subjects. There has also been a disproportionate focus on the "bubble kids," due to this testing, to the exclusion of those at the very bottom and our advanced learners. Some of the students at the bottom have been written off as hopeless cases. It is assumed that our advanced learners will make it without additional assistance. Either assumption could be construed as constituting educational malpractice.

The nation needs to restore a full curriculum that includes the humanities and the arts, and those subjects must be honored. The notion all students need to attend a four-year college or university to be successful in life must be reconsidered. In Finland, where students are perceived to be among the most highly functioning in the world, the curriculum is balanced and students engage in a well-rounded curriculum through the tenth grade. At that point, they either pursue a college track or a vocational program. While 53 percent enter the college track, a full 42 percent enter vocational training (Sahlberg, 2012).

There is absolutely no stigma attached to the vocational curriculum in Finland. Students pursuing this path typically enter well-compensated and satisfying jobs. Decisions about curriculum in Finland are jointly made by local community councils (similar to our school boards), working in conjunction with the local teachers and administrators. Rather than pursuing a common core type of curriculum, these groups decide what is best for their communities. There is little doubt that this approach contributes greatly to that nation's 95 percent high school graduation rate.

When the author was an instructional director in Colorado, two of his district's high schools were pursuing a creative approach to vocational education, offering such courses as applied physics and applied mathematics. One teacher was even able to entice a company to donate a hovercraft to that school's science department. Through the instructor's relationship with the United States Air Force Academy (he often invited in Air Force Academy instructors as guest lecturers) he was able to have the hovercraft flown from Florida to Colorado Springs. The final step involved having a local company deliver the hovercraft from the airport to the school in one of its delivery trucks. The intent of these programs was to channel students into some postsecondary education, but not necessarily the traditional college track. In today's test-based accountability climate, establishing such programs would be quite difficult.

While the author was a public school superintendent, he was able to work with staff to initiate elementary strings programs in two separate districts. The board of education in one of the districts even saw this as a recruiting tool and felt it would attract parents supportive of education to our school district. It was not unusual for parents in that region to "school shop" before deciding where to purchase a home. Due to the current focus on the basic curriculum as well as the continual struggle with finances, the implementation of such arts programs is likely to be rare. Scarce district resources are more likely to be spent on in-service training in the NCLB tested areas.

When the author was the superintendent of a district in central Illinois, he worked with a number of middle school staff members and a high school science teacher to establish an environmental habitat adjacent to the district's elementary and middle school buildings. This was located in a rural area, and in addition to the seventeen acres the school district was able to donate to this project, the district also leased an adjacent forty acres to expand the site. In addition to planting native prairie grasses and trees, the district constructed a pond, and because of the existence of a nearby creek, a riparian habitat area was also included. The author's major contribution to the cause was grant writing to help with the seed money for the project. This became a large source of community involvement, with many volunteers participating in the Prairie Creek Environmental Habitat. Such a venture would not be a high priority in many of today's districts.

Reducing school size is another way to address the academic performance of students. While this is an economic issue, it is a concept to be considered. The largest high school in Finland is fifteen hundred students and most elementary schools and middle schools enroll approximately three hundred students (Sahlberg, 2012). Every Finnish school has a child welfare team that immediately targets struggling students in the school. Many American schools have a similar team, but if a school is too large, there is a greater chance of students falling through the cracks. An intermediate approach taken by some U.S. schools is to break schools into villages or houses in order to reduce the number of students being educated or otherwise dealt with by each adult.

Ways need to be found to ensure the nation's very best teachers and administrators work in the lowest-performing schools and districts. This concept is completely contrary to the U.S. model of education. Often, teachers and administrators begin their careers teaching the basic courses or working in struggling schools. As they gain skill and experience, they attempt to move into higher-level courses; perhaps honors and Advanced Placement, or in the case of administrators, into more affluent schools. Creative thinkers need to find ways to entice the best teachers and administrators into the neediest schools, and to make the educational profession more attractive as a whole. The United States has a system where nearly half of all teachers exit the profession within the first five years. In Finland, less than 15 percent of educators leave the profession during their entire careers.

Within the past few years, programs such as Teach for America (TFA) have received a fair amount of notice in the press. The young people participating in TFA have often graduated from the very best universities, and are often liberal arts majors, or have majored in specific subject areas rather than teacher education. While it appears some of these individuals initially have a fair degree of success with their students, their attrition rate is on a par with teacher education graduates. There is no doubt the education profession needs to solicit and enroll the very best teaching and administrative candidates possible. It is also certain that teacher preparation and administrator preparation programs must be upgraded.

A few years ago the author presented a paper at a foreign conference where he addressed the struggles of the U.S. educational system. One of his recommendations was to consider pay incentives for teachers and administrators working in underachieving schools. He was roundly criticized by some in the audience for making this suggestion. His critics strongly believed that individuals should take on such roles because they are committed to working with young people in such environments rather than for a larger paycheck. While this sounds good in theory, it is not practical in the current world of U.S. education. While money may not be a motivator in the long term, it can be used to entice educators to consider a situation they may have otherwise discounted.

The author's first principalship was in an economically depressed community where the school's free- and reduced-lunch program had a count of approximately 90 percent. Residing within that community were a few doctors and dentists who were working there in order to excuse their medical school loans. States should consider similar arrangements to bring in excellent teachers and administrators for at least a period of time. Not just any teachers and administrators are being suggested. Rather, the very best candidates should be identified and supported financially throughout their training programs. These teachers and administrators should be educated in programs specifically designed to improve the chances of success for working in such schools and districts. Not only should their school loans be excused in exchange for a set number of years' work in such communities, but their pay should be significantly enhanced throughout their tenure in such districts.

The pay of teachers and administrators should be increased in general. Ways must also be found to break the grip of the standardized salary schedule and to reward and encourage the very best educators. Some districts, such as Denver, have experimented with this approach. Returning one more time to the Finnish example, teachers in that country are held in as much regard as medical doctors and engineers and salaries are excellent. There is an 80 percent confidence level for teachers among the Finnish public. This is due largely to the great success of the Finnish system; a system that is not judged by standardized test scores. There is little doubt that much of the success of the Finnish system comes from the rigor of teacher selection and the strength of their teacher training programs.

Some would say it is much easier to pay Finnish teachers more, because there are so few teachers when compared with the United States. Add to that the very high tax rate of 40–50 percent for most individuals, and you can see how high salaries are possible. Would anything like this even be possible in the United States? When you consider the population of Finland, at about 5.5 million, is analogous to some U.S. states, and remembering that education is theoretically a state function in the United States, then this vision may no longer be totally out of reach. The path forward would be made easier if states would shift the tax burden away from property taxes and enhance other forms of taxation. Concurrently, federal tax dollars could be redirected to enhance the compensation of teachers and administrators in high-need areas.

Returning to the possibility of differentiated salary schedules, the role of teacher unions must be considered. The unified salary schedule has been a bedrock principle of teacher unions for over forty years. Recent legislation in several states in conjunction with states' desires to gain RTTT funding may have inflicted a small chink in the armor of teacher unions. Some states now mandate at least a portion of each teacher's evaluation will be tied to student performance, a concept that would have been unthinkable even a few years ago. In some states, it has become easier to dismiss less-than-stellar teachers. While teacher unions are on their knees, they may be more amenable to discussing alternative paths to promoting excellence. Unions may determine increased flexibility, such as in the area of teacher compensation, to be in their best interests if they are to remain relevant.

In order to achieve any of the dreams just listed, administrators must regain their role as spokespersons for the U.S. public education system. Part of the strategy for regaining the initiative in this area means redefining what accountability in education means to the American public. Administrators have been too naive, too timid, or too busy doing other things to combat their loss of authority as the educational experts. This role has been taken over by private individuals and organizations and by state legislators and federal officials. What can be done to restore administrators to their rightful role as the advocates for a strong public education system and once again exert a positive influence on the system?

STRATEGIES FOR RECOVERY

The first thing administrators need to do to recover the initiative is to be much more positive and to work together with all other educators. Many U.S. schools and school districts are actually doing an excellent job of educating American students, and the best U.S. students are competitive with the top students across the globe on the international tests used to compare students. Administrators have allowed schools to be judged by a very narrow definition of accountability, a definition confined primarily to how well students perform on annual assessments in specified areas. A major irony of the NCLB system is that the actual assessments and indicators of success vary from state to state. According to this definition of accountability, all students are to be achieving at 100 percent by 2014. This assumes that all students are equally capable, and have the same advantages as all other students.

There was a valid reason for concern when NCLB was authorized. It was discovered that various subgroups were not performing up to par with the nation's mainstream, usually majority, students. Shame on educators for allowing this to happen. Yet, rather than establishing a logical system for addressing the situation, such as a growth model, the "one-size-fits-all" NCLB approach was implemented. Instead of allowing states to truly address the problems that were uncovered, as would seem to be logical in a state-controlled system of education, the nation received the present model. Public trust had been eroded so much since the publication of *A Nation at Risk* that states acting through their proxies, the local school districts, were not given the opportunity to address these problems utilizing local approaches.

A major key to winning back public support is to take every possible opportunity to share the positive things happening in public school buildings and school districts. Alternative means of accountability must be shared with the constituents of the public education system. Rather than focusing exclusively on state-mandated assessments, other nationally standardized tests utilized by districts should be highlighted. When a scholar bowl team or a Math Counts team wins a district, regional, or state contest, this should be widely publicized. When students perform well on Advanced Placement examinations, the public must be informed.

Additionally, National Merit semifinalists and finalists should be made known to all in the region. Student participation in Model UN activities and increases in the number of students enrolling in advanced mathematics and science courses should all be points of pride. Student recipients of scholarships to universities and technical schools of all types should be prominently noted in the media. Note student matriculation at prestigious institutions of higher learning. Highlight service academy appointments.

School and school district quality is also reflected by student participation in a whole range of student activities. While athletics generally receive the most attention, many communities are known for their music and other performing and visual arts programs. These are also signs of excellent schools and districts, because these activities build skills and character for productive citizenship. Related to this is student involvement in service and volunteer activities in their communities. Bringing community members into the schools on a regular basis will also enhance the schools' public image.

If anything, many schools and districts have been guilty of being too modest regarding the accomplishments of their students, teachers, administrators and other employees. Many of us have the sense that we are only doing our jobs. However, if we do not share our successes with the public, it is unlikely that anyone else will take primary responsibility for that task. It pays to consciously develop and maintain a positive relationship with the local media in a school community. It seems the media is always there when something negative transpires in a school or in a district.

It is also true that many experienced administrators have been frustrated when the press does not appear to cover a positive event, even after a special invitation. However, educators must keep trying in that regard. School principals and superintendents must establish specific goals for improving and increasing media contacts and relationships. One positive strategy is to assign a specific individual in a building and in a district as the designated media contact. Becoming the media's "go to administrator" in a region is a means of spreading positive information about public education.

The author's experience has been that that willingness and ability to publicly share successes may be regional in nature. In Illinois, he heard for years how great things were north of I-80. This was in reference to the fact that many of the wealthier suburban areas of the state were north of Interstate 80. Reports in central and southern Illinois indicated that the northern region of the state was where one would find the "land of milk and honey." At the end of his administrative career, the author accepted a superintendency in Lake County, which is adjacent to the Wisconsin border.

While his new school district was excellent, as were most in the region, many of the districts were no stronger or more sophisticated than the districts in other regions of Illinois. The northern districts simply had a much better public relations apparatus in place and their constituents believed they lived in superior school districts. This positive feeling certainly paid off at referendum time. The author also found a similar positive public relations approach in the district he served in Colorado Springs. That district had a central office administrator in that district who spent a portion of his time as public relations director. A person played a similar role in the district in which the author worked in the state of Washington.

The author once read information from the National School Public Relations Association (NSPRA) to the effect that it takes up to thirty positive events to overcome one major negative event in a school district. Many of public education's wounds are self-inflicted. It is critically important for every administrator at every level to work with both support and certificated staff to present a positive image of the school district. This is not to say if negative or unethical events in a school district are transpiring, they should be covered up. However, if individuals are complaining for no legitimate reason, they should be reminded of the source of their paycheck. There is a great deal administrators can and should do to build pride in their buildings and their districts.

The author learned during many referendum attempts as a central office administrator and superintendent that support staff members are often at least as important to any referendum attempt as teachers and administrators. In many school districts, a larger proportion of support staff lives in the district than do certificated employees. Thus, these individuals are more likely to have the ear of the voters than their certified counterparts. The same is true regarding all types of district issues, so be aware of the sentiments of these individuals. It should also be noted these individuals also are likely to be a source of information for school board members, particularly in smaller districts.

One of the most important advances that can be made in the battle to regain the initiative is to present a unified front as educators. This means teachers, and their unions, must work with administrators and school board members to advance the cause of public education. This initiative must also include parent leaders, such as PTA and PTO officers, booster club members, and so on. As administrators, everything must be done to ensure the best people possible pursue positions in public education. This means building principals employ the best certificated and support staff possible and they encourage the strongest parents to become actively involved in leadership positions. As a superintendent, this means encouragement of strong parents and community members, to the extent practical (perhaps through minions), to become involved in board service.

Encouraging unions and school board members to work together is likely to be a very difficult task, and the initiative for promoting constructive interactions between these two groups will probably fall to administrators, since they are in the middle of the organizational structure. Even though the superintendent serves as the CEO for the board of education, it is often up to the superintendent to help the board see the union's point of view. This often happens during collective bargaining, where it is left to the superintendent to remind board members that eventually the negotiations will end and a contract will be ratified. After the ratification, all parties will find it necessary to once again work together. While it may occasionally be difficult for teacher union members to forgive and forget, this is often more difficult for board members. Some school board members view the collective bargaining process as "game playing" and do not understand how professional educators can behave in such a fashion.

One approach some districts have used to improve union-board relations is "win-win" negotiations. In this process, the negotiation teams for both sides begin the process with joint training. Part of the rationale for this training is for the members of the teams to get to know one another. When the process actually begins, the two sides share interests, rather than proposals. They move on to brainstorming exercises and eventually begin to narrow and discuss their interests. While this is certainly not a panacea, it has the potential of establishing more positive working relationships in some districts.

Earlier in the book, the need for a district action plan was discussed. The development, distribution and implementation of this type of instrument can be used as a team-building exercise for the district, as well as an excellent public relations device. Rather than having only the board of education and administration develop the action plan, involve staff members as well. Why not solicit a bit of community input while you are at it? By all means, post the action plan on the district website as well as distributing it through other means. When progress on the plan is reported to the board of education, post these updates on the website and provide them to the press. This should become an excellent communications device promoting positive feelings throughout the district and community.

Form positive relationships with municipal, state, and national politicians. Many of these officials already know the private individuals and groups attempting to influence public education. Administrators at all levels should form similar positive relationships with these individuals. This can be done in many ways. Attend their fundraisers and make at least a token contribution, regardless of party.

If legislators represent an administrator and that administrator's school district, a relationship must be developed with those lawmakers. Invite state legislators and congressional representatives to regional administrative meetings and ask them to give legislative updates. This is also a way to hold a conversation and ask questions in a fairly nonthreatening manner. Do not be shy about giving legislators, in particular, specific input regarding pending legislation. Be certain to give a specific analysis regarding how such legislation would impact the school district, and the legislators' constituents.

Administrators should reach out to the parents in their schools and districts and to other constituents for their advice and suggestions regarding educational programs. Do this through public meetings, surveys, and one-on-one conversations with community leaders. One of the largest mistakes in this arena is waiting until referendum time to initiate outreach efforts. Administrators put on a full-court press in the months leading up to election day, and then return to a normal mode of operations. Working to establish positive relationships with constituents should be a full-time effort in every school and every school district in this nation. This should become a part of the fabric of each educational institution and must become second nature; schools and districts should come to be known as listening institutions.

Another way to improve relationships with the community is to get as many people as possible into schools. Invite the community to music and drama productions. Give reduced-cost or free passes to athletic events to senior citizens. Involve seniors in activities such as grandparents' days, even if they are not the biological grandparents of your students. Do not be afraid to bring in community members as volunteers. In some states, it is legal to give senior citizens property tax reductions for volunteering in the schools and after the seniors complete their required hours of service, some continue volunteering without compensation.

The author worked with a large number of building principals over the years, and was always fascinated with their differing attitudes regarding the use of volunteers in buildings. Some embraced volunteers with open arms and made great use of these individuals. Others wanted nothing to do with "outsiders" coming into their buildings. At times, principals with the negative attitude had been influenced by their teachers regarding volunteers and in other instances, the principals suppressed the requests for volunteers by the teachers. While it is understandable some principals are philosophically opposed to the use of nonprofessionals and others do not wish to invest the time to properly train these individuals, administrators need to consider the political and accountability aspects of such involvement.

This is not a case where absence makes the heart grow fonder. The more time noneducators spend in public schools, the more positive they will become. It also must be remembered administrators are accountable to the public as educators, not just through the board of education. One of the reasons so many magnet schools, laboratory schools, and private schools have such great parental and community support is because constituents are expected to volunteer in those schools. Increased constituent participation in schools is inexpensive and provides great benefits to the system.

One of the things learned by many administrators is an angered constituent may become the district's next school board member. This is not to imply that administrators should live their lives in fear. Conversely, many school board members come from the ranks of school volunteers, thus it is not unusual for PTO officers, booster club members, and referendum committee members to subsequently run for the school board. While administrators must be judicious in supporting candidates, all administrators can be involved in the grooming process. When an administrator recognizes a talented parent or other community member with board potential, that individual should be appointed to a school or district committee. Get the individual involved, and then set the hook. If school and district administrators are to return to prominence as educational experts, this must be accomplished arm in arm with competent and informed school board members.

The author was truly blessed during his eleven years as superintendent to work with many excellent school board members. There was only one true "stinker" during his tenure as superintendent. However, there are districts with long histories of ineffective or contentious boards of education. Changing the culture in such districts will be difficult, but it is necessary lest all be painted by the negative brush of such board behavior. A strong and competent superintendent can influence and change these board members. Unfortunately, such boards typically do not search for strong superintendents. In such cases, the change in these boards may need to be more grassroots in nature.

One strategy for improving and educating existing boards of education is a board-administrative retreat. The author held one or two of these a year during his last two superintendencies. Typically, two evenings in a particular week would be set aside for these retreats. Initially, these retreats were held in the early summer, before the building administrators went off duty. The board members liked these so well the board requested a second retreat, to be held in late January or early February. These retreats allow the administrative team and board of education to address philosophical issues at length and in a level of detail that is not possible in regular board meetings.

All district administrators should be included in these retreats, including assistant principals and deans. This enables board members and junior administrators the chance to establish closer relationships than would otherwise be the case. Each retreat can address six to ten major topics over the two evenings. Do not pack the agenda too heavily or there will not be sufficient time to address each item in detail. Specific administrators and board members should be assigned to lead the discussion on the various agenda topics.

Retreats should be great team-building exercises. Begin each evening with a nice meal and then move into the business of the evening. One thing to remember is that in most states, such retreats are considered to be board of education meetings and should be posted as such. If it is anticipated that union officials may attend the retreat, some items may be listed for the "closed session" on the agenda. In many states, all board meetings must be held either within the district or at a location "convenient" to district residents.

Boards of education can also be improved through staff development provided through state school board associations. In many states, the state organization will hold regional meetings throughout the state for board members with excellent professional development items on the agenda. Some states require board members to participate in a few hours of professional development activities during their terms of office. Some states allow a board of education to go into closed session with a representative of the state school board organization for board self-assessment and improvement activities. An annual convention for school board members is held in a few states, and the National School Board Association also holds an annual conference.

If administrators are to win the battle for educational primacy they must work closely through their professional organizations and support their lobbying efforts. Administrators need to become personally involved and contribute to these organizations in a leadership capacity whenever possible. This may run counter to the nature and beliefs of some administrators. Some administrators may wish to devote their time exclusively to their schools and districts. There may have been a time when this was possible, but that time is long past. All administrators must take accountability for being aggressive in this regard.

While the lobbying efforts of these professional organizations have impact, the level of funding generated by these groups is still far below what is provided by some private individuals and special interest groups. Administrators may question whether the effort is worth the time devoted and the money spent. The author regularly invites the chief lobbyist for the Illinois Association of School Boards to speak to his doctoral classes in Politics and Policymaking in Education. The lobbyist addresses this very issue and says that legislators do notice and appreciate the contributions from such groups. Such efforts keep us on the playing field of influence.

A BUCKET LIST

There is room for improvement in all public schools and school districts. Most, however, are serving their clients very well, in spite of what is reported in the press. At the same time, some U.S. schools are failing; especially some urban schools in economically depressed areas. As long as this happens, the nation will fall short of its potential. While inferior facilities and materials can have an impact in these communities, the real deficit is often the quality of teachers and administrators in these schools. Most of these individuals are committed and hardworking educators, but they may not be up to the task they face. These failing schools need the very best teachers and excellent administrators to move them forward.

Some states have occasionally taken over failing school districts, often under provisions of NCLB. In other cases, cities with school districts under mayoral control have tried a variety of approaches to improve urban districts. Chicago is one such example. Several years ago, Chicago moved to school committees, ostensibly to give parents direct control over their schools. At the same time, the central authority of the district recently made the decision to close a large number of schools deemed to be underperforming. A Chicago-based scholar, Pauline Lipman has written extensively about the struggles of the Chicago schools, and claims the actions of the central authority are designed to provide schools only capable of providing employees for the service industry in Chicago.

Remaining in Illinois, the Illinois State Board of Education has taken control of a handful of public school districts in the attempt to improve their schools. One district, East St. Louis District #189, has now been under state control twice since 1994. Still, the district's students continue to struggle academically. When the state takes control of any district, it effectively disenfranchises the voters of that school district. The situation in East St. Louis is unique, but indicative in many ways of the struggles facing similar districts nationally. This is not an easy situation to resolve.

The first step is to get the right teachers and administrators into those school districts.

Also on the bucket list is the recommendation for the nation to invest much more heavily in education. The proposal is not the indiscriminate throwing of money at school districts. Rather, the government should fund research addressing the best means of addressing the issues of urban schools. Pilot projects should also be funded, based on promising research results. Governmental scholarship programs and student loan forgiveness programs should be established and provided to the very best teacher education and administrative candidates willing to commit to working in the neediest schools and districts. The government could provide supplemental bonuses to educators remaining and providing effective service in such districts.

Teacher training and administrative preparation programs need to be enhanced, with specialized training for those candidates intent upon working in struggling districts. Related to the previously addressed government-sponsored research addressing effective practices for struggling schools, teachers and administrators must be given the tools necessary in order to bring about meaningful improvement in these districts. Certainly, face-to-face experiences with students in poor urban districts must be an expectation of such programs. Undoubtedly, enhanced student teaching experiences and expanded and improved administrative internship programs are necessary. In a statewide survey of Illinois superintendents that the author conducted with three colleagues in 2011, not one superintendent indicated that his or her administrative internship had been too easy.

Several states have recently revised the requirements for their principal preparation programs, since the principal is considered to be a key player in the school improvement process. One of the proposals in Illinois during its revision process was a full-time paid internship for principal candidates. Since virtually all candidates for the principalship and the superintendency are also working full-time in their day jobs, they work in their internships around their other duties, usually in their own schools and districts. A paid internship, which would release them from their duties, would be a great step forward. This would also enable administrative interns to engage in more diverse experiences.

It was estimated that the cost of supporting full-time principal internships in Illinois would be approximately $10 million annually. Is that so unreasonable? That concept was quickly eliminated, and although the ad hoc committee of administrators and professors called together to give advice to the state regarding changes needed developed several excellent suggestions for improvement, many of these were ultimately eliminated by state board staff in favor of bean-counting approaches to improvement. The reversal of recommendations from administrative practitioners was another sign of state board of education officials' lack of respect for public school administrators. This same lack of respect exists in many states today.

Through whatever means required, administrators must regain their status as the educational experts in this country. This is still a challenge, considering the huge sums of money being spent by private individuals and groups in the effort to influence educational policy. Thus far, their funding efforts have been very effective. These individuals and groups must be fought through a national grassroots effort whereby educators of all stripes rebuild relationships with their constituents, community members, and legislators. Unless public education can be restored as the preferred option for most Americans, this nation will be permanently altered as a truly democratic entity.

When the author was a superintendent, he frequently talked about public education being a partnership consisting of three components. This partnership was likened to a triangle, or a three-legged stool. One leg, or point, consisted of the home, another point, or leg, was the school, and the final portion was the community. The home had to send students to school ready to learn, and the school had to take every student, wherever that student happened to be academically, and help the student progress academically. The community had the responsibility to financially and philosophically support the schools in their community. In other words, the community needed to have the schools' back; a situation that exists in some communities, but not in others.

WHERE DOES ACCOUNTABILITY RESIDE?

Accountability for the quality of public education resides with all members of American society. As just recounted, the home, the school, and the community all have responsibility for public education. Educational administrators, specifically, are accountable to multiple groups. Beginning with building-level administrators, they are first and foremost accountable to the students in their buildings. This accountability means much more than students making AYP as prescribed by NCLB.

Yes, administrators must accept responsibility for the academic achievement of students in their buildings, and such progress can figure in to administrative evaluations if conducted properly. However, judging administrators on student progress should be addressed through a growth model rather than arbitrary standardized percentages. Additional measures of accountability should be used to judge the success of building administrators. The composition of the student body must be taken into account when measuring accountability, and administrators must be provided with the proper tools to enable success in this critical educational venture. Student academic progress must be a key factor in administrative accountability, but it also must be understood all playing fields are not level; at least not initially.

Building administrators should be accountable to students in several additional ways. All students must be handled with an ethic of care in mind. Students should be encouraged to learn and school must be a safe environment for all students. It should not be forgotten school is the best experience of the day for many students. School-level administrators are accountable for ensuring students are educationally challenged each day.

Administrators frequently underestimate what students are capable of achieving if properly motivated and challenged. Building administrators are accountable for providing the types of student activities and auxiliary experiences that build student character and competence in fields other than those deemed strictly academic. Finally, and perhaps most importantly, building administrators must be accountable for making school fun for students. Yes, school should be fun. Too many adults have forgotten what it was like to be a child and need to encourage creativity rather than smothering it in the name of academic growth.

Principals and other building administrators are accountable to students and parents for providing the best staff possible to conduct the educational process. This means administrators must have a clear vision of the type of teachers and support personnel they need in their buildings. The recruitment and hiring process must be taken seriously. Building administrators may not have as much influence over this process in some districts as in others. However, administrators must continually lobby the human resources department or the district office for a particular type of teacher that meets their needs.

Principals and other building administrators are accountable to their teachers and support staff members for creating a situation that enables those individuals to totally focus their efforts on the education of children. Everyone in the organization should be considered a support person to the teachers in the classroom. This includes everything from reducing classroom distractions to providing the supplies and materials necessary for those in the classroom to do their jobs effectively. This includes the provision of appropriate curricular materials. Building administrators are also accountable to teachers and support personnel to provide proper staff-development activities.

Principals and other building-level evaluators are accountable to students and parents for guaranteeing the best teachers possible are placed in each classroom. If a teacher is performing in a less-than-satisfactory manner, then that teacher must be remediated or removed. Too many ineffective teachers have been given a pass over the years because building administrators thought it would be too much work or too confrontational to engage in a remediation process. Others feared, or knew, that they would not have the support of their superintendents and school board members. Administrators must always keep the interests of students in mind in these situations.

Building-level administrators must be held accountable for addressing their district's vision and goals and must be team players. At the same time, they are accountable for giving the best advice and information possible to district-office administrators. Building administrators are also accountable to their peer administrators in other buildings. A bit of friendly competition among buildings is fine, but such competition can be destructive if it becomes too intense. More than anything else, building-level administrators must take care of one another.

Building-level administrators are accountable to the public and must ensure all aspects of their buildings are run ethically. This includes supervision of money, staff, and academic honesty. It is easier for a building-level administrator to run afoul of the law over money than a superintendent, because building administrators handle money on a daily basis. Administrators must immediately investigate any report of staff misbehavior, especially as it pertains to students. All students must be treated fairly in every aspect of school operations, including discipline, class placement, and so on.

Building-level administrators are accountable for following the chain of command as a matter of practice. There are times when it is appropriate for principals to speak directly with school board members, but this should normally be done with the superintendent's knowledge. This also implies that building administrators should be contributing members of the district's administrative team. As such, they should do nothing to undermine the work of the team. Administrators must also encourage their teachers and other staff members to appreciate and adhere to the chain of command.

District-level administrators below the superintendent are accountable to the superintendent, especially if they are in a line position reporting directly to the superintendent. These district-level administrators are also accountable for providing the best programs possible under their areas of supervision. These administrators are also accountable to the entire administrative team and must be contributing members of that team. Like the building-level administrators, district administrators are accountable to the district vision and goals. These district administrators are also responsible for promoting the ethic of care in their districts. While these individuals may not have daily contact with students, they do exercise control over district procedures that influence how students are treated. There are times when such district administrators are accountable to the board of education; particularly if they have been assigned a specific project to complete for the board.

Superintendents are accountable to the world. At least, it seems that way at times. First, superintendents are accountable for providing the strongest education for all the students in their districts, not just the state scholars and honor students. Superintendents are also ultimately accountable for ensuring the ethic of care becomes ingrained in the culture of their school districts. Superintendents are accountable to parents and guardians for the safety and care of their children. Superintendents are accountable for making certain district resources are properly channeled to do the most good for the students of their district.

Superintendents are accountable to the teachers and support staff in their districts regarding their working conditions. Building staff must have the proper materials, building leadership, and training to do the best job possible for their students. In this regard, superintendents, working with principals, must guarantee teachers they have the strongest colleagues possible. If a teacher or support person is not working up to par, the superintendent must wholeheartedly support the building administrator's efforts to remediate or remove that individual. This is critical to other staff members and to students.

Superintendents are accountable to building-level and district administrators to adequately integrate them into the district's culture. When a subordinate is off path in any area, or is in jeopardy with the board of education, the superintendent must be that individual's best loving critic and support that administrator's improvement efforts. The superintendent is accountable for building and maintaining a strong board-administrative team in the school district. The superintendent is also accountable for overseeing the development of a district vision and strategic plan. These activities must be accomplished in partnership with board members, employees, and constituents.

The superintendent is accountable to the board of education and his or her fate is ultimately controlled by the board. However, the superintendent has major accountability or responsibility for board training. The superintendent is often the mediator between the board and the troops in the district. The superintendent, more than anyone else, can influence the quality of the board of education. The superintendent is accountable for treating all board members equitably regarding the flow of information, support, and so on.

The superintendent is accountable for giving the board the best advice possible in all areas, understanding the board may accept or reject that advice. However, the superintendent must not shy away from sharing the best counsel possible with the board. The superintendent is also accountable for keeping the board of education informed regarding all areas of significance within the district. One excellent technique in this regard is to provide each board member with weekly written updates. These updates typically include anywhere from a half dozen to perhaps a dozen items, which should include the good, the bad, and the ugly. No board member likes to be surprised, especially if the news is bad. It is impossible and foolish to keep bad news from board members.

The superintendent is accountable to the larger community. The superintendent must keep the community informed regarding the school district's achievements, struggles, and needs. If the district is struggling academically, the superintendent must not hide this from the community but must share a vision of how the district will move forward. The same is true if the district is encountering fiscal difficulties. The superintendent must use all available means available to communicate with the community.

Finally, all building- and district-level administrators are accountable to the profession of public education to continually advocate for this approach to educating the nation's youth. Working individually and through their professional organizations, educational administrators must work to regain the trust and support of the public for the American system of public education. This need not be done by bashing private and parochial schools, charter schools, or those homeschooling their children. Rather, this will be a process involving rolling up sleeves and working together to change the public perception of public education. No educational administrator can any longer attempt to avoid this battle.

A VOICE FROM THE FIELD

It is easy to become depressed over the media's portrayal of public education. It seems many state legislatures have abdicated their responsibility for adequately funding the public education system. The fiscal problems in many states were created by the actions of past legislatures failing to adequately fund education or by raiding public teachers' pension systems. Some state budgets are now being balanced by sacrifices of current and retired educators and other state employees. The call for accountability, based almost exclusively on student performance judged by test scores, adds to the stress level of current educators.

Just as the author was able to improve his disposition as a building or district administrator by visiting the classrooms of excellent teachers, he maintains hope for the future because of the quality of the individuals enrolled in principal and superintendent preparation programs. There are still many very high-quality individuals out there in the field, doing an excellent job for their students and their districts. While these individuals occasionally have a "down" day, they are essentially optimistic about the future. After all, without optimism, what is the hope for the future? Fortunately, many excellent educators are still interested in pursuing a career in educational administration.

The author is also encouraged by many of the fine administrators he worked with over his career. A vast majority of these individuals were much more effective and competent than the picture painted of educational administrators in the press. These were strong individuals who were not afraid to face difficult situations. One elementary principal, in particular, was willing and able to develop a remediation plan for a teacher with twenty years of teaching experience. Over a period of more than a year, she devoted countless hours beyond her normal workday on this situation. Ultimately, the teacher resigned from the district, thus improving the prospects of countless incoming first graders.

It is incumbent upon experienced educational administrators to inform the upcoming generation of administrators there is life beyond NCLB. These administrators must realize accountability takes many forms and cannot truly be reduced to standardized test scores. While assessments of student achievement should not be ignored, administrators must consider a range of additional assessments and measures of accountability. Are students challenged and happy? Are they progressing? These should be the keys to accountability.

SUMMARY

In this chapter, the constant calls for accountability for educational administrators were discussed. These have led to increasing levels of stress, and administrators seem to continually be in a defensive posture. It was stated accountability is necessary, but accountability with multiple definitions. Alternative definitions for accountability were given for educational administrators playing different roles in the educational system. It was also asserted the U.S. public educational system is much stronger than its public image.

All calls for accountability must ensure students receive the best education possible, not just an education based on standardized test scores. A return to a more comprehensive curriculum, including sufficient attention to the humanities, the arts, and vocational education, was recommended. Reducing school size as a means of paying more attention to individual students was strongly suggested, even though this would come with a financial cost. Administrators must provide an ethic of care that addresses the needs of all students in their schools and districts. Administrators must work as members of administrative teams to help move their districts forward.

It was deemed essential for the best teachers and administrators to be employed in the nation's struggling schools. This runs counter to current practice, where the goal is often for the best teachers to move into higher-level courses or into more affluent districts as they progress in their careers. Administrators frequently follow the same path. It was suggested tuition waivers, forgiveness of student loans, and enhanced pay for working in struggling schools would be options for helping place the strongest educators in the neediest situations. It was additionally recommended sufficient federal funding should be redirected to help meet these needs. Another recommendation was for the federal government to fund university research regarding effective instructional and administrative techniques for implementation in struggling and urban schools.

The nation received NCLB for a reason. Clearly, students in some subgroups were not academically achieving on a par with their peers in other subgroups. Rather than addressing this in a creative fashion, the country received a carrot-and-stick approach to accountability—mostly the stick. Educational administrators must seek ways to inform the national discussion regarding accountability and to show there are many ways to judge the quality of schools and school districts. Failure is not an option if this nation is to retain its promise as a democratic society.

Educational administrators must build a unified front. This includes working together with educators from all levels, forming relationships with municipal, state, and national politicians, and encouraging more people to actually visit our schools. Administrators also need to work to ensure the quality of local boards of education is as high as possible. Finally, administrators must work through their professional organization and actively engage in lobbying efforts to win back their status as the rightful spokespersons for public education. The road ahead will be difficult and challenging for educational administrators, but there is no other choice if public education is to survive. The grassroots effort must begin today.

References

Anderson, M. (2007). Principals and conflict management: Do preparation programs do enough? *Journal of Scholarship & Practice, 4*(1), 4–13.

Anyon, J. (1997). *Ghetto schooling: A political economy of urban educational reform.* New York: Teachers College Record.

Barker, R., Pearce, C. G., & Johnson, I. (1992). An investigation of perceived managerial listening ability. *Journal of Business and Technical Communication 6,* 438–57.

Bielick, S., Chandler, K., & Broughman, S. (2001). *Homeschooling in the United States: 1999.* Jessup, MD: ED Pubs (ERIC). 1–34.

Brown v. Board of Education, 347 U.S. 483 (1954).

Brownell, J. (1990). Perceptions of effective listeners: A management study. *The Journal of Business Communication, 27*(4), 401–415.

Brunner, C. C. (2002). A proposition for the reconception of the superintendency: Reconsidering traditional and nontraditional discourse. *Educational Administration Quarterly, 38*(3), 402–431.

Buck, R., Miller, R., & Caul, W. (1974). Sex, personality, and physiological variables in the communication of affect via facial expression. *Journal of Personality & Social Psychology, 30*(4), 587–596.

Bush v. Holmes, 919 So. 2d 392, 398 (Fla. 2006).

Carr v. Koch, 2012 IL 113414.

Center for Research on Education Outcomes (CREDO) (2009). *Multiple choice: Charter school performance in 16 states.* Stanford, CA: CREDO, Stanford University.

Citizens United v. Federal Election Commission, 558 U.S. 310 (2010).

Coleman, J., Campbell, E., Hobson, C., McPartland, J., Mood, A., Weinfeld, F. & York, R. (1966). *Equality of educational opportunity.* Washington, DC: U.S. Department of Health, Education and Welfare.

Collins, J. (2001). *Good to great: Why some companies make the leap and others don't.* New York: Harper Collins.

Collom, E. (2005). The ins and outs of homeschooling: The determinants of parental motivations and student achievement. *Education and Urban Society, 37*(3), 307–335.

Colorado League of Charter Schools. (2013). *Charter School Facts.* Retrieved April 21, 2013, from www.coloradoleague.org/colorado-charter-schools/charter-schools-fact-sheet.php.

Committee for Educational Rights v. Edgar, 672 N.E. 2d 1178 (Ill. 1996).

Darling-Hammond, L. (2003). Access to quality teaching: An analysis of inequality in California's public schools. *Santa Clara Law Review, 43,* 101–239.

Darling-Hammond, L. (2004). Standards, accountability and school reform. *Teachers College Record, 106*(6), 1047–1085.

Darling-Hammond, L. (2006). Securing the right to learn: Policy and practice for powerful teaching and learning. *Educational Researcher, 35*(7), 13–24.

Darling-Hammond, L., & Bransford, J. (2005). *Preparing teachers for a changing world: What teachers should learn and be able to do.* San Francisco: Jossey-Bass.

Dawkins, M. & Braddock, J. (1994). The continuing significance of desegregation: School racial composition and African American inclusion in American society. *Journal of Negro Education, 63*(3), 395–405.

Diamond, J., & Spillane, J. (2004). High stakes accountability in urban elementary schools: Challenging or Reproducing Inequality? *Teachers College Record, 106*(6), 1145–1176.

Drollinger, T., Comer, L., & Warrington, P. (2006). Development and validation of the active empathetic listening scale. *Psychology & Marketing, 23*(20), 161–80.

English, F. (2010). The ten most wanted enemies of American public education's school leadership. *International Journal of Educational Leadership Preparation, 5*(3), 1–9.

Foley, R., & Lewis, J. (1999). Self-perceived competence of secondary school principals to serve as school leaders in collaborative-based educational delivery systems. *Remedial and Special Education, 20*(4), 233–243.

Fritts, J. (2012). *Essentials of Illinois school finance: A guide to techniques, issues, and resources.* 6th. ed. Springfield: Illinois Association of School Boards.

Frost, E. A. Jr. (1987). A descriptive study of the academic achievement of selected elementary school-aged children educated at home in five Illinois counties. Doctoral dissertation, Northern Illinois University, 1987.

Galloway, R. (1995). Home schooled adults: Are they ready for college? Paper presented at the Annual Meeting of the American Educational Research Association, San Francisco, CA.

Green, C., & Hoover-Dempsey, K. (2007). Why do parents homeschool? A systematic examination of parental involvement. *Education and Urban Society, 39*(2), 264–285.

Gulosino, C., & Liebert, J. (2012). *Review of the way of the future: Education savings accounts for every American family.* Boulder, CO: National Education Policy Center.

Haas, J., & Arnold, C. (1995). An examination of the role of listener judgments of communication competence of coworkers. *Journal of Business Communication, 32*, 123–139.

Haycock, K. (2001). Closing the achievement gap. *Educational Leadership, 58*(6), 6–11.

Hernandez v. Texas, 347 U.S. 475 (1954).

House, R. (1996). Path-goal theory of leadership: Lessons, legacy, and a reformulated theory. *Leadership Quarterly, 7*, 323–352.

Hunt, J. (2006). Impact of the failure to make adequate yearly progress on school improvement and staff development efforts. *Connexions.* Posted November 6, 2006, at http://cnx.org/content/m14097/latest.

Hunt, J., & Morice, L. (2008). Where race intersects community: The case of Lehew v. Brummell. *Journal of Philosophy and History of Education, 58*(1), 92–97.

Hunt, J., Watkins, S., Kersten, T., & Tripses, J. (2011). Restructuring (retooling) superintendent preparation programs to enhance district leadership. *Education Leadership Review, 12*(3), 61–66.

Hunt, J., Kim, J., Watkins, S., & Tripses, J. (2013). *School board presidents' recommendations for superintendent preparation programs: Community influence through shared governance.* Paper accepted for presentation at the Annual U.C.E.A. Convention held in Indianapolis, IN.

Illinois State Board of Education. 23 Illinois Administrative Code, 30.30 General Program Requirements 37 Ill. Reg. 4258.

Jehn, K. (1995). A multi-method examination of the benefits and detriments of intragroup conflict. *Administrative Science Quarterly, 40*, 256–82.

Johnson, L. (1965). President Lyndon B. Johnson's Commencement Address at Howard University on June 4, 1964, *To fulfill these rights.*

Jones, P., & Gloeckner, G. (2004). First-year college performance: A study of home school graduates and traditional school graduates. *The Journal of College Admission* (Spring), 17–20.

Justice Policy Institute (2002). *Cellblocks or classrooms? The funding of higher education and corrections and its impact on African American Men.* Retrieved February 20, 2012, from www.justicepolicy.org/article.php?id=14.

Konnert, M., & Augenstein, J. (1990). *The superintendency in the nineties: What superintendents and board members need to know.* Lancaster, PA: Technomic.

Kotlyar, I., & Karakowsky, L. (2006). Leading conflict? Linkages between leader behaviors and group conflict. *Small Group Research, 37*, 377–403.

Kowalski, T. (1999). *The school superintendent: Theory, practice and cases.* Englewood Cliffs, NJ: Prentice Hall.

Kumashiro, K. (2008) *The seduction of common sense: How the right has framed the debate on America's schools.* New York: Teachers College Press.

Kurtzleben, D. (2012). National debt interest payments dwarf other government spending. *U.S. News World Report,* November 19, 2012. Retrieved February 10, 2012 from www.usnews.com/news/articles/2012/11/19/how-the-nations-interest-spending-stacks-up.

Ladner, M. (2012). *The way of the future: Education savings accounts for every American family.* Indianapolis, IN: The Friedman Foundation for Educational Choice.

Ladson-Billings, G. (2006). From the achievement gap to the education debt: Understanding achievement in U.S. Schools. *Educational Researcher, 35*(7), 3–12.

Lambert, L. (2006). "Half of teachers quit in 5 years." *Washington Post,* May 6, 2006.

Lehew v. Brummell, 103 Mo. 546 (1890).

Levin, H., & Rouse, C. "The true cost of high school dropouts." *New York Times,* January 25, 2012.

Lipman, P. (2004). *High stakes education: Inequality, globalization and urban school reform.* New York, NY: Routledge.

Litchka, P., & Polka, W. (2013). Consensus v. conflict: Dilemmas in decision making for school superintendents. Paper presented at the 2013 AERA Meeting in San Francisco, CA, April.

Locke v. Davey, 540 U.S. 712 (2004).

Loveless, T. (2008). "An analysis of NAEP data." In *High achieving students in the era of NCLB* (pp. 13–48). Washington, DC: Thomas B. Fordham Institute.

Maes, J., Weldy, T., & Icenogle, M. (1997). A managerial perspective: Oral communication competency is the most important for business students in the workplace. *Journal of Business Communication, 34,* 67–80.

Mendez v. Westminster, 161 F.2nd 774 (9th Cir. 1947).

Mooney, A., Holahan, P., & Amason, A. (2007). Don't take it personally: Exploring cognitive conflict as a mediator of affective conflict. *Journal of Management Studies, 44*(5), 733–755. Oxford, UK: Blackwell Publishing.

Morice, L., & Hunt, J. (2008). By the numbers: Attendance laws and inequality of educational opportunity in Missouri, 1865–1905. *American Educational History Journal, 34*(2), 275–287.

National Commission on Excellence in Education (NCEE). *A nation at risk: The imperative for educational reform* (Washington, DC, 1983).

Natriello, G., McDill, E., & Pallas, A. (1990). *Schooling disadvantaged children: Racing against catastrophe.* New York: Teachers College Press.

No Child Left Behind (NCLB) Act of 2001, Pub.L. No. 107-110 (2002).

Orfield, G., & Lee, C. (2005). *Why segregation matters: Poverty and educational inequality.* Cambridge, MA: The Civil Rights Project at Harvard University.

Parents Involved in Community Schools v. Seattle School District No. 1, 551 U.S. 701 (2007).

Plucker, J., Burroughs, N., & Song. R. (2010). *Mind the (other) gap! The growing excellence gap in K–12 education.* Bloomington: Indiana University, School of Education, Center for Evaluation & Education Policy.

Priem, R., Harrison, D., & Muir, N. (1995). Structured conflict and consensus outcomes in group decision making. *Journal of Management, 21*(4), 691–710.

Race to the Top (RTTT) Program (2009). American Recovery and Reinvestment Act (ARRA) of 2009, Pub.L. No. 111-5 (2009).

Rakestraw, J. (1987). An analysis of home schooling for elementary school–aged children in Alabama. Doctoral dissertation, University of Alabama–Tuscaloosa, 1987.

Ray, B. (1990). *A nationwide study of home education: Family characteristics, legal matters, and student achievement.* Salem, OR: National Home Education Research Institute.

Ray, B. (2011). *2.04 million homeschool students in the U.S. in 2010.* Salem, OR: National Homeschool Research Institute.

Rentner, D. S., Scott, C., Kober, N., Chudowsky, N., Chudowsky, V., Joftus, S., & Zabala, D . (2006). *From the capital to the classroom: Year 4 of the No Child Left Behind Act, Summary and Recommendations.* Washington, DC: Center on Education Policy.

Rothstein, R. (2004). *Class and schools: Using social, economic, and educational reform to close the black-white achievement gap.* Washington, DC: Economic Policy Institute.

Rudner, L. (1999). Scholastic achievement and demographic characteristics of home school students in 1998. *Education Policy Analysis Archives 7.*

Sahlberg, P. (2010). *Finnish lessons: What the world can learn from educational change in Finland.* New York: Teachers College Press.

Sahlberg, P. (2011). Lessons from Finland. *American Educator* (Summer), 34–38.

Schofield, J. (2004). Fostering positive intergroup relations in schools. In J. Banks & C. Banks (Eds.), *Handbook of Research on Multicultural Education* (2nd ed., 799–812), San Francisco, CA: Jossey-Bass.

Strauss, R., & Sawyer, E. (1986). Some new evidence on teacher and student competencies. *Economics of Education Review, 5*(1), 41–48.

Teale, W., Paciga, K., & Hoffman., J. (2007). Beginning reading instruction in urban schools: The curriculum gap ensures a continuing achievement gap. *The Reading Teacher, 61*(4), 344–348.

Thomas, K. (2002). *Introduction to conflict management: Improving performance using the TKI.* Mountain View, CA: CPP, Inc.

Thomas, K., & Kilmann, R. (2007). *Thomas-Kilmann conflict mode instrument.* Mountain View, CA: CPP.

Wartes, J. (1990). Recent results from the Washington Homeschool Research Project. *Home School Researcher, 6,* 1–7.

Watkins, S., Hunt, J., & Tripses, J. (2012). Learning effective listening skills: Implications for superintendents. Paper presented at the 19th International Conference on Learning, London, England.

Watkins, S., & Sheng, Z. (2008). Are state and national standards leaving the advanced learners behind? The crisis ahead. *Forum on Public Policy.* Retrieved February 22, 2013, from http://forumonpublicpolicy.com/summer08papers/archivesummer08/watkins.pdf.

Wells, A., & Crain, R. (1997). *Stepping over the color line: African-American students in white suburban schools.* New Haven, CT: Yale University Press.

Wheatley, M. (2006). *Leadership and the new science: Discovering order in a chaotic world* (3rd ed.). San Francisco, CA: Berrett-Koehler Publishers, Inc.

Wolfe, B., & Haveman, R. (2001). Accounting for the social and non-market benefits of Education. In J. Helliwell (Ed.), *The contribution of human and social capital to sustained economic growth and well-being* (pp. 1–72). Vancouver: University of British Columbia Press.

Wyner, J., Bridgeland, J., & Dilulio, J. Jr. (2009). *Achievement trap: How America is failing millions of high-achieving students from lower-income families.* Rev. ed. Lansdowne, VA: Jack Kent Cooke Foundation and Civic Enterprises. Retrieved February 22, 2013, from www.jkcf.org/news-knowledge/research-reports/.

Xiang, Y., Dahlin, M., Cronin, J., Theaker, R., & Durant, S. (2011). *Do high flyers maintain their altitude?* Washington, DC: The Thomas B. Fordham Institute.

Zelman v. Simmons-Harris, 536 U.S. 639 (2002).

Index

academic challenge, 31
Academic Yearly Progress (AYP), 3–4, 7, 15, 109; bubble kids, 5
accommodating, 65, 67, 73
accountability, v–vi, 114; bubble approach, 5; building level management, 110–111; Chicago Public Schools policies, 7; decision making and, 58; district-level administration, 111; listening skills and, 78; locating, 109; principals, 110; standardized tests and, 29; state-developed tests and, 3–4; superintendents, 111–113; teacher education programs, 110; teacher preparation and, 29
achievement gap, 18
ACT, 43
active empathic listening, 79
active listening, 79
administrative accountability, v, 1; growth of, 67–68
administrative preparation programs, 108
administrative training: in certification renewal, 71; conflict resolution needs, 69, 73; decision making, 69, 73; people skills, 69–70
administrators: academic achievement responsibility, 109–110; conflict management, 59; conflict resolution strategies, 63; conflicts faced by, 60; decision making sharing by, 57–58; decision making skills, 59; feedback to, 67; increasing pay, 99; media contact with, 102; subordinate communication with, 90–91; use of listening skills, 80
advanced placement classes, 6–7, 98, 101

affective conflict, 59, 63–64
African Americans, 7, 13, 19–20, 76–77; in charter schools, 46; dropout rates, 25; mathematics courses and, 24
AFT. *See* American Federation of Teachers
Alexander, Lamar, 2
alternative certification, 28
American Federation of Teachers (AFT), 29
American Recovery and Reinvestment Act (ARRA), 1
Arizona, 39
Arizona Empowerment Scholarship Accounts, 39
ARRA. *See* American Recovery and Reinvestment Act
arts programs, 97
avoiding, 65, 67, 73
AYP. *See* Academic Yearly Progress

board-administrative retreats, 106
boards of education: conflict resolution strategies of, 65; conflict with, 62–63; improving, 106; staff development, 106; superintendents meeting with, 89; teacher quality and, 30
Broad, Edythe, 48
Broad, Eli, 48
Broad Foundation, 48
Broad Residency in Urban Education, 48
Broad Superintendents Academy, 48
Brown v. Board of Education, 12, 19–20, 31
Brummell, William, 19
bubble approach, 5
bubble kids, 4–5, 15, 96

Index

Budget Reduction Advisory Committee, 89
building level management, 2–3, 110; accountability of, 110–111; central-office administration conflict with, 61–62; conflicts faced by, 60–62; organizational structure, 60
Bush, George W., 7
Bush v. Holmes, 39
Business Roundtable, 48
busing, 12

Carr v. Koch, 11
Cato Institute, 48
CCSSO. *See* Council of Chief State School Officers
Center for Research on Education Outcomes (CREDO), 45–46
Center for the Study of American Business, 48
central-office administration, building-level administration conflict with, 61–62
charter schools, v, 36, 44, 52, 54; in Colorado, 45; legislation of, 53; minority students in, 46; in Missouri, 44; performance research, 45–46; UNO, 45
Chicago Public Schools, 7, 44–45, 48, 107
Citizens United v. Federal Election Commission, 37
Cleveland, 38
Clinton, Bill, 2
cognitive conflict, 59, 63–64
Coleman Report, 22
collaboration, 55, 65–66, 73
collaborative decision making, 55, 68, 72
Collins, Jim, 58
Colorado, 30, 39, 52, 53; charter schools, 45
Colorado League of Charter Schools, 45
Colorado Springs, 51, 85, 88, 97
Colorado Supreme Court, 39
Committee for Educational Rights v. Edgar, 10–11
community college classes, 43

community groups, conflict with, 63
community involvement, 104–105
community meetings, 88
competency levels, 6
competing, 65–66, 73
comprehensive curriculum, 96–97
compromising, 65–66, 73
conflict, 56–57, 59, 72; affective, 59, 63–64; with board of education, 62–63; building-level management, 60–62; cognitive, 59, 63–64; in decision making, 56–57; employee, 61; intra-office, 62; management of, 59; with parents, 60–61; school district budgets and, 77; with students, 60–61; superintendents facing, 61–63; types and sources of, 60
conflict resolution, 57, 59, 73; administrative training needs in, 69, 73; modes of, 65–67, 73; strategies, 63; training in, 70–71
Confluence Academy, 44
consensus building, 55–57
conservative religious groups, 77
constituent groups, 87–89
constructive conflict, 56
Council of Chief State School Officers (CCSSO), 49
CREDO. *See* Center for Research on Education Outcomes
Crispus Attucks School, 31
curriculum gap, 24

Darling-Hammond, Linda, 23, 25, 27
decision making, 55, 72; accountability and, 58; administrators sharing, 57–58; assigning power for, 57–58; collaborative, 55, 68, 72; conflict in, 56–57; consensus building, 55–57; skills, 59; stress and, 68; training in, 69, 73
delegation, 58
destructive conflict, 56
detached listening, 79
Devos Foundation, 49
differentiated salary schedules, 100
disabled students, 77
distributive leadership, 83

Index

district action plans, 103–104
District Advisory Committees, 86–87
district-level administration: accountability of, 111; conflict in, 62; conflict resolution strategies of, 65
district organizational structure, 11
dropout rates, 25–26
dual credit options, 6
Duncan, Arne, 48

East St. Louis schools, 107
EAV. *See* Equalized Assessed Valuation
Edison Project, 48
education: equitable, 25; increased difficulty in jobs in, 95; intergenerational effects, 21; investment in, 108; nonmarket effects, 21; as three-way partnership, 109. *See also* public education
Educational Savings Account (ESA), 36–37, 39, 53
Education Commission of the States, 49
education debt, 18, 31–32
education reform movements, 1, 37; creativity lost through, 8; Excellence Movement, 1, 15; Restructuring Movement, 2, 15; Standards Movement, 3, 15
Education Trust, 25
effective listening, defining, 78
elementary strings programs, 97
ELL. *See* English Language Learner
employee conflicts, 61
English, Fenwick, 48
English Language Learner (ELL), 4, 46
environmental habitats, 97–98
Equalized Assessed Valuation (EAV), 9
equitable education, 25
ESA. *See* Educational Savings Account
ethic of care, 84
ethic of justice, 84
Excellence Movement, 1, 15

Finland, 14, 26–27; curriculum in, 97; school size in, 98; teacher pay in, 99; teacher turnover in, 28

Finn, Chester, 48
Finnish Lessons: What Can the World Learn from Educational Change in Finland? (Sahlberg), 26
fiscal inequality, 9, 14
Florida, 38–39
Florida Supreme Court, 39
foundation-level education funding approach, 17, 32
Friedman, Milton, 37
Friedman Foundation for Educational Choice, 37, 39

Gerstner, Louis, 48
government scholarship programs, 108
grade-level centers, 11–12
Gregorc Style Delineator, 65
Grundy County, Missouri, 19
Gulosino, Charisse, 39

Haycock, Kati, 25
Heritage Foundation, 22, 49
Hernandez v. Texas, 20
Hess, Frederick, 48
highly qualified teachers, 24, 45
High Objective Uniform State Standard of Evaluation (HOUSSE), 24
high-stakes tests, 7, 78
homeschooling, v, 36, 40, 51–52, 53; demographics of, 40; interscholastic activities and, 42; parents and, 41; reasons for, 40–41; regulation of, 41–42; socialization activities and, 43; standardized achievement tests and, 42–43
honors classes, 6
Hoover Institution, 49
HOUSSE. *See* High Objective Uniform State Standard of Evaluation
Howard University, 21
HURIER model, 79

IASA. *See* Illinois Association of School Administrators
IBM, 48
Illinois, 52; charter schools, 44–45; online training mandated by, 96; principal internship proposal in,

108; SAELP and, 49–50; SREB and, 50; superintending mentoring in, 69; teacher evaluation in, 96; Wallace Foundation and, 49–50
Illinois Administrative Code, 50
Illinois Association of School Administrators (IASA), 69
Illinois Association of School Boards, 107
Illinois Constitution, 10
Illinois SAELP (I-SAELP), 49–50
Illinois State Board of Education (ISBE), 11, 49–50, 107
Illinois Supreme Court, 10–11
income disparity, 14; academic performance and, 14; standardized achievement tests and, 22
induction programs, 27
Industrial Revolution, 53
intergenerational effects of education, 21
International Baccalaureate programs, 6
internship period, 27
interscholastic activities, 42
intra-office conflicts, 62
involved listening, 79
Iowa Tests of Basic Skills, 43
I-SAELP. *See* Illinois SAELP
ISAT, 5
ISBE. *See* Illinois State Board of Education

Jackson County, Texas, 20
Jindal, Bobby, 50
John Olin Foundation, 49
Johnson, Lyndon B., 21

Kennedy, Anthony, 13
Kilmann, Ralph, 65

laboratory schools, 52
Ladner, Matthew, 39
Ladson-Billings, Gloria, 18, 31–32
Latinas/os, 20, 76–77; in charter schools, 46; dropout rates, 25
leadership, 57; distributive model, 83; transactional, 63–64; transformational, 63–64

Lehew v. Brummell, 19
Liebert, Jonah, 39
Lipman, Pauline, 7, 107
listening: audiences, 89; defining, 78; models of, 79, 93; navigating difficult situations through, 84; phases of, 80–81; processing in, 79, 80–81; types of, 79
listening skills, vi, 75–76, 92–93; accountability and, 78; gender differences in, 76, 82, 93; generational attributes and, 82; importance of, 75–76; improvement of, 80; of principals, 90–91
literacy support, 22
lobbying efforts, 106–107
Locke v. Davey, 38, 53
low-income communities, 99
low-income families, 22; recession and, 77; vouchers and, 39
low-income schools, 22; curriculum gap, 24–25; teacher expectations in, 25; teacher turnover in, 23
lunch programs, 77
Lynde and Harry Bradley Foundation, 49

magnet schools, 13, 36, 52, 91–92
Manhattan Institute, 49
Marshall, Thurgood, 20
Math Counts, 101
mathematics: advanced, 24; homeschooling and, 42; minority students and, 24
media coverage, 102
Mendez v. Westminster, 20
mentorship programs, 27
merit pay, 29
Mexican Americans, 20
middle-class schools, 23
Milwaukee, 37
minimum competency levels, 6
minority enrollment mandates, 12
minority families, 76–77
minority students: in charter schools, 46; income status, 22–23; mathematics courses and, 24; standardized achievement tests and, 22

Missouri, 19, 52; charter schools, 44
Missouri Supreme Court, 19
mock interviews, 70
Model UN, 101
Mouth Counts, 7
"Multiple Choice: Charter School Performance in 16 States" (CREDO), 45–46
Myers-Briggs Type Indicator, 65

NAACP, 20
National Association of State Boards of Education, 49
National Conference of State Legislatures, 49
national debt, 18
National Education Association (NEA), 29
National Governors Association, 49
National Merit Scholars, 101
National School Board Association, 106
National School Public Relations Association (NSPRA), 102
National Teacher Examination, 29
A Nation at Risk, v, 35, 101
Native Americans, 20
NCLB. *See* No Child Left Behind Act
NEA. *See* National Education Association
negative modeling, 92
negotiated agreements, 23, 60
neighborhood-school concept, 11–12
neoliberalism, 48, 54
"90/90/90" schools, 22
No Child Left Behind Act (NCLB), v, 3, 5, 7–8, 14–15, 95, 100–101, 107, 109, 114–115; achievement gap and, 18; creativity lost through, 8; curriculum narrowing under, 96; education debt and, 18; highly qualified teachers and, 24, 45; open enrollment and, 36; Title I program and, 4, 8; waivers, 6
"no excuses" schools, 22
nonmarket effects of education, 21

open enrollment, 36
Opportunity Scholarship Program (OSP), 38–39

parents: conflicts with, 60–61; homeschooling and, 41
Parents Involved in Community Schools v. Seattle School District No. 1, 13, 16
passive listening, 79
Phi Delta Kappa, 35
Plessy v. Ferguson, 19
Prairie Creek Environmental Habitat, 98
"The Principal Internship: How Can We Get It Right?" (SREB), 51
principals: accountability of, 110; conflict resolution strategies of, 64; evaluation of, 62, 85–86; feedback to, 67; high-stakes evaluation of, 78; internship programs for, 108; listening skills of, 90–91; preparation programs, 108; superintendents' conflict with, 62; teacher quality and, 31
professional organizations, 106–107
property taxes, 9, 11
public education, 35; accountability and, v, 113; business management model, 35; creativity in, 8; criticism of, 35; homeschooling and attitudes towards, 40–41; neoliberal attacks on, 48, 54; perceptions of, 47–48; public support of, 35
public relations, 102

Race to the Top (RTTT), 1, 48, 51, 62, 78, 100
racial balancing, 13
Readers Digest, 49
Reeves, Douglas, 22
referendums, 88, 102
religious schools, 38
resegregation, v, 12
Response to Intervention (RtI), 8
Restructuring Movement, 2, 15
right to work, 30
Riley, Richard, 2
Rothstein, Richard, 22
RtI. *See* Response to Intervention
RTTT. *See* Race to the Top

SAELP. *See* State Action for Education Leadership Project

Sahlberg, Pasi, 14, 26
Sarah Schaife Foundation, 49
school boards, 103, 105
school desegregation orders, 12–13, 16
school district budgets: conflict with constituents and, 77; constituent group meetings about, 88–89; court challenges to inequality in, 10–11; federal money in, 8; fiscal inequality and, 9; residential housing patterns and, 10; revenue sources, 9
school improvement planning, 3, 15
school integration, 12–13
School Leader Task Force, 49
school quality, 101
school reform movement, 37
school size, 98
segregated neighborhoods, 13, 23
segregated schools, 22–23, 33
self-concept, 64
separate but equal, 19, 21, 33
shadow educational system, 36, 52
site-based management, 2
Smith Richardson Foundation, 49
socialization activities, 43
South Carolina, 27
Southern Regional Education Board (SREB), 49–51, 54
standardized achievement tests: accountability and, 29; homeschooling and, 42–43; income level and, 22; minority status and, 22
Standards Movement, 3, 15
Stanford Achievement Test, 43
State Action for Education Leadership Project (SAELP), 49
state-developed tests, 1; accountability based on, 3–4; homeschooling and, 42
St. Louis, 13
student loan forgiveness, 108
students: conflicts with, 60–61; disabled, 77; discipline issues, 60. *See also* minority students
student teaching, 27
superintendents: accountability of, 111–113; board of education conflict with, 62–63; board of education meeting with, 89; communication by, 82; conflict resolution strategies of, 65; conflicts faced by, 61–63; constituent group meetings with, 87–89; control of information, 83; employment decisions, 30; feedback to, 67; mentoring, 69; principals' communication with, 90–91; principals' conflict with, 62; teacher quality and, 30–31; teacher unions meeting with, 86

tax credits, 38
tax revenue, 9
teacher education programs, 27; accountability of, 110; alternative certification, 28; teacher preparation programs, 28
teacher quality, 23–24, 32; accountability for, 29; board of education influence on, 30; impact of, 27, 29; importance of, 26; internship and student teaching impact on, 27; mentoring and induction programs, 27; principals' roles in, 31; superintendents' roles in, 30–31; turnover and, 28
teachers: conflicts with, 60; evaluation of, 62, 78; expectations of, 25; high-stakes evaluation of, 78; increasing pay, 99; preparation programs, 28–29; training programs, 108
teacher turnover, 23; teacher quality and, 28
teacher unions, 23, 29–30, 86, 100, 103
Teach for America, 26, 28, 98
team building, 106
test result comparisons, 3
test-taking skills, 3, 96
Thomas, Kenneth, 65
Thomas B. Fordham Foundation, 48
Thomas-Kilmann Conflict Mode Instrument, 65–66, 73
Title I program, 4, 8; NCLB failure sanctions, 4, 8
transactional leadership, 63–64
transformational leadership, 63–64
trial balloons, 87–88
Truman, Harry, 57

two-class systems, v

unified salary schedule, 100
United States Air Force Academy, 97
university laboratory schools, 27
UNO charter schools, 45
U.S. Civil War, 19, 53
U.S. Supreme Court, 12–13, 16, 19–20, 37; voucher plans and, 38, 53

values education, 77
vocational curriculum, 97

volunteers, 105
vouchers, v, 36–37, 49, 53

Wallace, DeWitt, 49
Wallace, Lila Acheson, 49
Wallace Foundation, 49–50, 54
Wal-Mart Foundation, 49
Warren, Earl, 20
white flight, 13

Zelman v. Simmons-Harris, 38, 53

www.ingramcontent.com/pod-product-compliance
Lightning Source LLC
Chambersburg PA
CBHW030144240426
43672CB00005B/258